Faith
and
Family

Growing Up Poor in Rural Uganda

Vincent Ajuk

ISBN 978-1-7371144-0-6 (print)
ISBN 978-1-7371144-1-3 (ebook)

Contents

CHAPTER 1:
A Child Is Born Poor in Uganda

~~◇

THIS IS A message of hope, courage, and endurance as spoken by a mother's voice to her son and a father's voice to his son that would help shape his life and future. They also offered messages of perseverance, determination, kindness, forgiveness, seeing the humanity in people, hard work, love, fearing God, trust, ability to believe in yourself, listen to advice from people around you, exercising good judgment, and never giving up when you fail. This is also the story of a little boy born in abject poverty in rural Northern Uganda who has refused to be defined by the poverty in his background but instead accepted it, embraced his condition, and used his life experience as a motivating factor to achieve greatness in life for himself and the life of his family and the life of people in his community and the community around him.

On December 9, in the wee morning, a baby boy was born to the family of Bensy Apio and Naputal Ogwang in a rural village of Adwila Lira district county of Adekokwok. The child was born on the empty floor on a papyrus mat. The only bed Bensy Apio and Naputal Ogwang could afford to lay their precious child on was a papyrus mat made off elephant grass and spear grass, which is the dominant type of grass covering the Northern part of Uganda. The grass thatch house built with mud and covered by cow dung had no windows, no ventilators, no electricity, and no running water. The child was born in a dark room except for the firewood that filled the room with smoke while providing the only light that was used to help light the inside Grass thatch house during the delivery of the precious baby boy. Bensy Apio and Naputal Ogwang had no blanket to cover their baby. The only clothes they could afford to keep their newborn baby boy warm were pieces of his mother's clothing.

My mother described to me the moment she saw her precious beloved baby boy when he arrived in this world, she knew her baby boy was different and special from her other nine children. Mom said she was filled with joy and excitement, and she immediately gave thanks to the Lord for blessing them with such a wonderful gift of life. Dad was overcome with joy and that the Lord had again blessed him with another son fulfilling his long-held wishes and dreams for having another baby boy in the family. As my mother told me, my father also immediately gave thanks to God for giving them such a beautiful precious gift of life, and immediately Dad and Mom knew the Lord was by their side and both knew that because of their strong faith in God, their dreams in life would be fulfilled.

Photo: *my three nephew and their names are Omara, holding the black goat and Ajuk holding the yellow goat and Obia holding the striped goat. Goat-rearing helped them with school fees when they were growing up and will be sold in the market to earn them some income to pay for their education.*

Dad and Mom knew that their prayers had been answered by God because Dad needed a baby boy to help him on the farm, looking after the animals, such as goats, cows, and sheep. Mom and Dad said that immediately after I came from the womb, I opened my eyes, looked my mother straight in the eye,s and cried three times, which she said was interpreted in our Langi culture as resisting the idea of coming into the world to face poverty, and thereafter I kept quiet, and I continued to stare straight into my mother's eye. The nurse who was attending to my mother's birth was speechless and didn't know what to say because she had never seen a child born with the ability to look straight in somebody's eye and make eye contact with their mother for such a long time. The nurse was so amazed by my birth, and she made a comment to my mother that, "Of all the traditional deliver I have ever attended, I have never seen a child who can look at their mother straight to the eye for such a long time," and my mother she replied to her nurse, "This is my special blessed son who God has given me to lift me and my family out of the bondage of poverty."

After I had lived only a day in this world, my mother and father's joy quickly came to an end when they realized that the nurse had not done an adequate job of cutting and tying the umbilical cord, and it had begun to bleed uncontrollably. They had no means of transport to rush the baby boy to the hospital because the nearby community health center was six miles away. My mother told me the story with tears rolling down her cheeks as she recalls how close she came to losing her baby boy, and Mom said to me they covered their baby boy up with rags and pieces of cloth because they did not have clothes of their own. They began a six-mile journey to the health center, praying every minute that God would save their little child. My mother had lost a lot of blood as well from the delivery. She was very weak and could not walk a long distance, but because of the love of her special blessed son, she had to do what it took to keep him alive, a son she believed and had high hopes, dreams, and the expectation that he would one day lift her up and the family from the bondage of poverty.

My mother said she was weak and couldn't walk a long distance, but, at the same time, her mind was telling her she had to because failure to keep going would result in the death of their blessed precious baby boy where all their hopes and dreams for a better life lay, so she gathered the determination to walk with all her might, strength, and the energy she had left in her and to persist with the sacrifice only a mother can make for the love of their children. My mother told me, "I prayed to the Lord to raise me up from the dust I was sitting on and give me the strength and the energy to walk a long distance to save the life of my blessed beloved precious baby boy." Mom said she continued to recite this prayer over and over in her mind, and with that simple hope, Mom believed God was by her side and gave her all the energy and strength to carry on walking the six miles distance to the health care center and she continued walking to save the life of her baby boy, the sacrifice only a mother can make in the love of their children. Another hurdle that my mother had to overcome was that she could not produce breast milk to feed her baby because she had not eaten food for many days, and there was little water to drink at that moment in their village. Back then, Mom and Dad and the people in their village had to walk many miles to fetch clean drinking water for their family. This made walking long distances difficult. You could hardly find any place where you could stop by and get clean drinking water for one to drink.

When Mom told me the story, I could hear the pain in her voice, and she said that back then there were no other ways to feed the young newborn children. In those days, all the newborns depended on their mother's breast milk. Mother said when she couldn't produce the breast milk to feed her precious baby boy, she prayed to her almighty father to come to her rescue at that desperate moment because she was helpless and there was nothing she could do but to trust the Lord to overcome the mountain in front of her and her husband and prayed to God to perform a miracle as Jesus did in the wilderness when he was able to feed the multitudes with a single loaf of bread and one fish.

At that moment, she asked my father for a prayer and a blessing and both knelt and prayed together before they began the six-mile journey walk to the health care center that they hoped would save the life of their baby boy. Immediately after the prayers, Mom told me something came to her in the form of a vision and told her to drink some water and that the water she drank would turn into milk to feed her newborn and that nothing would happen to her child. She drank the water, and a little breast milk came, and she was able to feed her son and gain the energy needed to allow her to walk six miles to the health care center to help save the life of her baby.

Mother said the journey to the health care center took them seven hours because she was weak and dehydrated. She had lost a lot of blood and water during delivery so that she could only walk for ten minutes or fifteen minutes and take a deep breath and rest under the tree to gain strength to allow her to take another step in a long journey to save the life of their child. Mother said she repeated the same routine during their journey to the health care center. She said she did not know where she got all that strength and the energy to carry on, but what kept her going was her faith in God and the prayers. Mom strongly believes that their faith in God help them overcome all the challenges that they were going through, and God guided them all along the way making sure whatever they asked for in prayers was fulfilled. Mom and Dad believed the prayers she made with my father before they began their journey to the health care center were answered by God, and he granted them the ability and wisdom to carry on with unmatched strength to carry on.

Mother said the love and the support of my father were paramount to her determination to carry on. She did not want to feel she let down my father the loved of her life. The blessed baby boy was being carried by hand by my father with no breast milk to feed him. Father had milked the cow at night and saved the fresh warm milk from the cow and carried it along with him in the journey, but he lacked the proper feeding bottle to feed his precious baby son so when the precious baby boy cried, a drop of milk and water was put in his mouth to feed him. Father and mother did not have a feeding bottle to feed the baby so they used a cup and a spoon-shaped leaf to put a drop of cow's milk to the mouth of their infant, also my mother and father said what they did know was that they need to keep the cup and local made leaf shape spoon and the container for the milk very clean so that the bacteria and the germs are kept away to prevent the baby getting any infection and falling sick. My Mother and Father were clean people. They did not have much at all, but the little they had was kept clean and proper to prevent her family from getting sick from germs and infections that the germs caused.

When my mother and father finally reached the health care center there was no one available to attend to their dying baby who they believed the child had lost almost all the blood and water in his body and was completely dehydrated due to lack of water and breast milk. The infant was in dire need of immediate attention to be put on the drip to add water and blood in his system to save his life. Mother and Father said there was a man on duty who came and spoke to them and asked them what was wrong with the child Mother and Father explained to him what the emergency was and why they had come to seek help for him.

Mom and Dad told me instead of the man coming to their rescue and helping their bleeding baby, the man asked them for money instead. The man wanted to know first if they had the money to pay to him first so that he will be able to assist their blessed precious baby. Mother and father said they both told the man that they were a very poor family that they could not even afford to feed themselves. Mom and Dad said they continued to plead to the man that they were hungry, with no food to eat, and that they have just walked seven miles to get to the health care center to get help to save the life of their blessed baby. Mother said she begged the administrator to save the life of their baby boy, but the man refused to help her instead he told them to look around and see how many people were in the waiting room seeking treatment, and some had already paid him money to be seen by that same man. Mom and Dad told me that the health care worker told them they are no different than those people who had paid him money already, and he continued to say they are not above everyone else who had paid him kickback money to treat them and if they failed to come up with the kickback, their child would not get medical treatment and when the man said that he then turn his back and walk away from them. Mother said the tears came rolling down her cheeks, seeing time slipping away from her baby boy. Immediately, Mother realized she needed to stay strong. No matter what happened, she would accept it. Mother and father again were faced with the reality of hopelessness and despair, and there was nothing they can do because they knew their only hope was that the health care center would provide the medical help their child needed to live.

Mother and Father again turned to their faith and their love of God. Mother said she asked Dad to kneel down and say a prayer for their little dying baby boy and for the Lord to bless the innocent pure soul for their little baby boy and also to ask the Lord for forgiveness for whatever wrong they have done in the presence of their Lord. Mother said she specifically prayed for compassion that the Lord would grant the workers at the health care center the compassion to help the sick and the dying. Mother also said she prayed for the Lord to grant the workers at the health care center empathy in their hearts to treat sick patients with respect and dignity at the time they need most in their life, and they said they prayed passionately for the will of God to come upon them and comfort them during the trial time in the hospital and grant them wisdom and ability to overcome the challenges that were before them the fear that they may lose their baby if he failed to get the medical attention he desperately needed.

Mother told me she prayed to the Lord to look upon her dying son and lift him up in his hand and heal him and send his angel to come and save her blessed beloved son. Immediately, she stopped praying and opened her eyes with my father kneeling beside her, and the other poor patients lying in front of her and looking at her and her husband. She saw the nurse come by, passing many sick patients in front of her, and unwrapped the baby and saw how sick he was, and she said to my mother how sick her baby was and that he needed immediate medical attention.

Mother told me how the nurse was struck by how good-looking the boy was. The nurse said, "This is a handsome baby boy," and immediately the nurse took the baby from their hands without asking how they would pay for the medical treatment because the nurses saw the condition of the baby was grave and that he could die anytime if the medical help is not administered immediately. The nurse put the baby on IVs to add blood and water to his system and a breathing tube to help the baby breathe more easily.

My mother and father said they stood near their baby boy helpless as there was nothing they can do only to continue to pray while the nurses work hard to save the life of their baby. Mother and father had a strong faith in God they knew from their heart that there was nothing impossible that God cannot do, they knew in their heart that the God of Abraham would not let their boy die. Their faith was so strong that they believed nothing would happen to their precious baby boy. With that strong conviction of faith, they were able to overcome their fear of the unknown and be able to stay strong regardless of what they were going through. When poverty collides with sickness, the ultimate price is death. This was true sixty years ago, and it is true now in Uganda and across the continent of Africa. After staying for a long time in the intensive care, with lots of blood and water added to his body, their baby started to gain consciousness and opened his eyes.

Mother and Father said that even made them pray even more to the Lord, to give thanks to their God, to ask for more blessings from their God, and to pray for all who were seeking medical assistance from the health care center because they could see the miracle happening before their eyes. Mother and Father knew their son was eventually going to die if he did not receive the medical help soon from the nurses, but at the same time, they believed in their faith, and they had hope that the Lord would not take the life of their child. They knew their God will not allow that to happen to them. Blessed are the poor they will find happiness in heaven, and they shall inherit the kingdom of God, and that was the lesson they learned from their church and kept in their hearts. Mother couldn't read and write, but she had a sharp mind, like a magnet. Once she learned something, it stuck in her mind forever. Mother could recite the verses in the Bible by heart, and I always wondered if she had been allowed to go to school by her father one would never know my mother would have been the person that would have helped her beloved child at the moment he needed help most. The words of comfort she learned from her church stayed in her brain and gave her comfort, strength, and peace of mind that their precious baby would be saved. Mother and Father kept their faith strong they never doubted God. They knew he is the one who gave life, they knew he would be the only one to take their boy from them when the time was right, and they were right it was not that time had not come.

Many weeks passed and the condition of their baby boy continued to improve every day. Mother and Father said after one month and one week in the intensive care the baby began to breastfeed. My mother said my father was overwhelmed with joy and gratitude for what a miracle the Lord had done for them. Mother and Father told me they saw a mother and a father crying every hour as their loved one in the health care center passed away simply because the medical staff could not save them because they lacked the means or the capacity to save the child's life. This is due to a lack of medical equipment and a lack of trained nurses and doctors to help save these precious lives that God gave us. Mother and Father said there were no beds or mattresses at the health care center. All the babies were laid down on the cement floor, which got very cold at night. There were no blankets for the patients, no food, no water, either cold or hot, and no electricity, of course.

Mother said they saw nurses treating patients with water, and sometimes nurses had to explain to the patients that there were no medications in the hospital, and the only option available is to treat them with water and hope that would heal the sick patient and sometimes patient developed swelling on their bodies due to too much water in their system. Mother and Father said sometimes they had to drink water for the day as food to sustain them. Mother and Father said some Good Samaritan at the health care center shared their leftover food with them. Mother said Dad went out every morning to work hard for people helping them to generate little money a day to buy them food to keep them in the hospital and help the remaining eight children at home. Mother said everyday father was by her side to keep her strong and give her encouragement and determination that all will be alright.

Dad did this after each day of hard manual labor, helping people and working in his garden to grow little food for mother and the eight little children left behind unattended in the mud house with no clean running water or electricity. Father had to travel seven miles back and forth every day to the hospital from the health care center to the village of Adwila to get food and water for the eight children left behind. Dad was a dedicated loving caring husband to our mother and his twelve children. Dad traveled fourteen miles round trip every day to the health care center in the village to make sure our mother and the other eight children are taken care of while my mother stayed in the health care center attending to their recovering baby boy.

Mother and Father said when the condition of their child improved, and it was time to discharge them from the hospital and the time to go home and take their bundle of joy home to their village of Adwila, they were again faced with another challenge: the health care center bill. The administrator demanded money from them. My mother and father again find themselves to the same situation they were in when they first arrived at the health care center because they did not have the money to pay the medical bills. Mother and Father again found themselves having to explain to the administrator that they did not have any money to pay, that they were very poor, and that they couldn't pay the health care center bill. After the administrator listened to Mom and Dad's explanation as to why they did not have the means to pay the health care center bill. The health care administrator was not pleased with their answer and immediately started to threaten my parents that he would keep the baby in the health care center until my mom and dad could come up with the ways and means to pay the bill.

Mother and Father were told by the health care center administrator to go back home and sell their animals, goats, and chicken to pay the health care center medical bills. Mom and Dad explained to the man that they did not have animals to sell. They only had goats and chicken and few cows to provide milk to drink for their nine children left at home with little food to eat. If they off their livestock, the eight children at home would have nothing to eat and their precious baby in the hospital would have nothing to feed him but the health care administrator did not want to hear that only what he wants is the money for the health care center. Mother and Father again turned to what they knew best and that was the power of prayer. Mom and Dad had a strong faith, and that faith guided them in all the decisions they made in their lives and the lives of their children. Their faith helped them a great deal in times of despair and hopelessness. They found comfort and solace in their faith, and they believed strongly that there was nothing that God cannot resolve, and it was that resolute determination that made Mom and Dad strong, and they were equipped with strength and determination to face the unknown with courage and without fear.

CHAPTER 2:
Grace Overcomes Greed

MOM AND DAD's faith made them immune to their suffering and poverty merely became part of their life. They accepted that they were poor, and they were determined to make good come out of their suffering. The only way they knew to make this happen was to do good for others and to see the good in humanity. Mom and Dad shared the little that they had with the many hungry souls in their community. Mom and Dad lived Christlike lives. Their souls were full of love, caring, sharing, laughter, and lifting people up who felt they cannot carry on anymore. Mom and Dad were the foundation and the pillars of our home. They taught us the value of family and how to cherish our family and love one another as we would want to be loved. Mom and Dad saw good in everyone, and they saw people as the beloved children of God, and as children growing up in a large family of twelve children, we were puzzled by what our Mom and Dad's acts of kindness to others were all about. We, as children, would always question why Dad and Mom were so kind to strangers and neighbors and why Mom and Dad are always happy, even if they were facing extreme hardship in providing for their twelve children, and we continued to ask Mom and Dad why they had to share the little they have with others even though they did not even have enough to feed twelve of us.

Mom and Dad never answered our questions directly. This was not just because they didn't want to answer these hard questions to their children but simply because they wanted us to emulate their act of kindness and be good children. First Mom and Dad wanted us to love ourselves and our sisters and brothers and learn from what they were doing by seeing their good deeds and their acts of kindness without their verbally communicating it to us. We, all the twelve children, were deeply touched by the ways our parents were being a good example to us all simply by their good deed in the community. We all learned how to love ourselves first and our brothers and sisters, and all twelve siblings loved each other. We learned the importance of sharing first among the twelve of us and then with others in our community who do not have much of what we have or have none. As these values continued to be ingrained in our minds, it became so clear to us twelve children that this is what our Mom and Dad would want to see in us growing up loving one another and the people around us. Treating people as we wanted to be treated, paying respect to the elderly and caring for them, treating neighborhood children as our brothers and sisters, and sharing with them the little we have with them.

I remember one day I was walking back from school, and I was very hungry and thirsty from school in my hands, I had one mango, which I was dying to eat so that I could quench my thirst and put something in my hungry stomach. When I was about two kilometers away from home, I reached another home in our neighborhood, and in that home, there were two young children, a brother and a sister playing in their yard. Upon seeing me, both children came running towards me, excited but also looking malnourished and pale. I saw the look of hunger in their beautiful faces, as these two children approach me politely and asked me if I could share my mango with them. They told me they had not eaten or drunk anything since morning and that their mother and father left very early in the morning to tend the family garden, and they had not come back to feed to them. It was around three in the afternoon.

I still remember the time vividly as it was today, looking at the children's faces and seeing what hunger and thirst were doing to their bodies. That day, I did not even hesitate one second to share my one mango with these two beautiful children of God. But remember, I was a child myself and very hungry and thirsty too, but because of the values my parents instilled in me at a young age to love our brothers and sisters the way we loved ourselves. Because of these good lessons and values, we learned from my Mom and Dad, the moment these two kids approached me to share my one mango with them, I didn't hesitate in a heartbeat to share my mangos with these children. I remember I didn't even mention to these kids that I had only one mango. All I did was to say to these kids was "Sure, if you want to share my mango, you are welcome to share with me."

As kids, we didn't have anything to cut mangoes into pieces so that we can share them evenly or equally, but even being without a knife didn't stop us from sharing our one mango. So, we came up with an idea of how we can share our mangoes equally without anyone of us complaining to one another about who got the largest piece. The idea was one person took one bite of the mangoes one at a time and pass the mango to the next person, and the process went on and on until the mango was finished, and the last person would save the mangoes seed and plant the seed in the ground to grow it.

I remember it was me who took the first bite of the mango and gave it to the next brother and the sister, and we continued to share the mango until the fruit was gone. Unfortunately, the mango was not big enough to fill the three hungry kids' bellies but was enough to contain our hunger. When I grew older, the memory experience never left my mind. I continue believe that it was the good thing I did to share my mango with those precious children, and that experience strengthened my desire to help those people who need help—the poor, the sick, the homeless, the blind, those with any form of disability.

You will always have moments in your life where you awaken humanity in yourself by doing something good for someone without any reservation in your heart and mind but out of only the feeling that it's the right thing to do at that moment and such kind act is so rewarding and fulfilling. As human beings, we must have empathy in our hearts and minds and that will always keep us human. I believe that because of acts of kindness, good deeds are done for us, and the lesson I learned from Mom and Dad at an early age has shaped my life to this day. I was able to see the humanity in people at an early age and learn to love everyone regardless of their age, color, or creed.

My mother and father believe all human beings are God's people created in God's image, and we should try to do our best to love everyone, even those who we may disagree with or the people who don't love you for reasons that you may not even know. At the same time, you can't stop people from not loving you, as human beings. We will always come across people who may not love us and may not have humanity in their hearts. They believe that everything that belongs to them and is theirs alone and not for anyone else. That is okay, as well, and they should not be judged.

Mom and Dad were loved in their community because their faith allowed them to see the humanity in everyone. Mom and Dad never discriminated against anybody, not the young, the elderly the poor, the sick, or the rich. All were God's children in the eyes of my mom and dad who must be loved and treated with respect and dignity. My parent fed hundreds of children with the little food they mother grow in their gardens. Mom and Dad knew and never doubted the Lord, and they knew that the Lord would help them overcome the challenge before them. Again and again, they turned to their faith and prayed that the health care administrator will have a change of heart and let them go home with their blessed beloved baby boy.

Mom and Dad knew that the Lord was always by their side for any given challenge placed before them, and they knew the way forward is to use the power of prayers and both knew that if they had prayed to the Lord with pure intent, the Lord would grant them what they were asking for, just as Mom and Dad began to pray to the almighty God to grant the health care center administrator a compassionate heart and allow them to go home with their baby boy without paying the bill because they were a very poor family, and there was no way they were going to find ways to raise enough money to cover the hospital bill. They also knew the Lord knows their heart and that they were telling the truth to the administrator, that they were poor and that they couldn't pay.

Mother said they were kept to the health care center for one day due to nonpayment of the bill, and the next day in the morning when the bright red sun of Uganda, Africa, came up, and the nurses and the health care center workers were reporting for duty in the morning. Mother and Father were sitting under the veranda of the health care center building with their blessed precious baby covered with rags. They saw the nurse that helped them when they first arrived at the health care center, seeking help for treatment for their baby boy. When the nurse saw them sitting under the veranda of the health care center, she asked Mom and Dad what was wrong and why they were still at the health care center since their son was doing well and had been cleared to go home.

Mother and Father then began to tell the story to the nurse that they are being withheld because of nonpayment of their bill, and they continued to explain to the nurse again as they did before when they were first admitted to the health care center that they do not have any means or capacity to because they were very poor family. Mother and father had finally found someone to advocate on their behalf with the hope that the administrator would listen to the nurse's explanation regarding their situation of not being able to afford the bill, being that they were coming from the poor village.

Again, the Lord had worked a miracle for my Mother and Father to rescue them from their bondage of poverty by sending the right full people to help them in times of their despair. According to Mom and Dad, their faith kept them strong and led them to freedom. Mother and Father always had hope in all that they did, despite the fact they were very poor, they never blame anyone either nor did they blame their God for being poor. Instead, they put their trust in God, and with that trust came strong faith which led them to the right path first in all what they did for themselves and to their children and for others. When Mom and Dad finished explaining their story to the nurse, she was filled with guilt and remorse and promised Dad and Mom that she would talk to the health care center administrator and see if he would have a change of heart and let free to leave with their baby.

After a few minutes, the nurse returned to my mother and father

to convey the good news message that the health care center administrator had a change of heart and cleared them and discharged them to
leave without paying the accumulated bills, and they were free to take
their healthy baby boy home. Mother and Father were filled with love
and joy in their heart that the Lord had saved the life of their child.
Mother and Father gave thanks to God, and they thanked the nurse
for saving their baby's life. Mom and Dad said they told the nurse they
were very appreciative for what the health care center did to help their
baby boy and above all they gave thanks to their almighty God for
sparing his life and for giving him a second chance at life.

When Mother and Father were being discharged from the health
care center to take their healthy baby home, the nurses realized my
mother did not even have clothes or a sheet for the baby or a clean
drinking cup. Mother and Father told the story of the nurses with
her tears coming down her cheeks. My parent told me how this one
particular nurse at the health care center helped them. Mom and Dad
said how this woman was so kind to them, just an individual nurse
who did all that she could to help them without asking for any favor
in return. She showed love and kindness to them and their little boy.
My Mom and Dad talked about how the nurse became their guardian
angel, cared for them, listened to them, gave them comfort at the times
they needed it most and make them feel that all was going to be okay
and that sense of compassion from the nurse renewed their faith and
allowed them to believe that there are good people out there who do
good work that the Lord calls them to do. Mother talked about how
her life story affected the nurse to the point that she was compelled to
do something to help my mother.

The nurse, with her compassionate, kind heart donated a baby sheet
to keep the baby warm when they got back home, and she also donated
her own clothes to my mother, so she'd have a change of clothes when
she got home. Mom and Dad could not stop talking about how God
works in mysterious ways where no one could know. God opened up
the heart of this nurse to be there for them. The next day Mother
and Father started their seven-mile journey walk back to their home
village, Adwila, to take their baby boy back home. After a long day of

walking from the health care center with the temperature near to over 100 degrees Fahrenheit with no shoes to protect their feet from the hot sand and no water to drink on their way, Mother and Father were tired and exhausted. When they finally arrived home, the people in their village were full of joy welcoming them back from the hospital. My mother and father were full of joy and thanked God, first for leading through that difficult time and second to their community for praying to God for keeping their precious baby alive, and now it was time to celebrate life and celebrate the birth of the boy born in the community of Adwila and to give him a name.

The community was joyful because they knew God had worked a miracle and to save the life of a child in the community, so all in the community came together to celebrate this precious life. The Langi tribe celebrates the birth of a child by preparing local beer made of millet flour and sorghum and locally brewed liquor called waragi, made of corn. These drinks are made in abundance to celebrate the occasion like birth, death, engagements weddings, and funerals. This is where the community comes together to eat, drink, and dance the traditional dances that go on all night, and the next day the blessed precious baby boy was finally given a name, Ajuk Ogwang, and the celebration continued all day. People ate and drink while celebrating the gift of life that God gave them, and the entire community loved one another and become one big family. At the celebration, big cows and goats and chickens are slaughtered to celebrate and mark the occasion.

Mother and Father choose the name because it meant a lot to them. It meant a person who had overcome all the odds against him and survived, a person who brings joy and happiness to people, a person with sound intellect and judgment, a person who will continue to serve his community, a child who will lead them and their community out of poverty, a leader who will unite people and is not a divider. What the names meant to my Mom and Dad, I will never know, but all that I do know is what my mother and father told me as to why I was given the name. When the name-giving celebration was over, it was time to welcome me to the family of nine children in which I was the ninth child and counting with eight sisters and an older brother. I was told my sisters were happy that I was born because they had another chance of having another younger brother to play with, and my older brother was happy as well because he got a younger brother to look after. My mother was blessed with five other children bringing the total number of our siblings to fourteen children ten girls and four boys unfortunately two girls died and brought our number down to twelve siblings, eight girls, and four boys. Mother and Father were very poor, but both my mother and father's hearts were full of love, caring, compassion, and gratitude towards all the people they met.

Mom and Dad both showed us unconditional love. My mother was the disciplinarian. She made sure all the twelve children grew up with respect and dignity, especially with respect for one another, respect for the elderly within our community, and the people we met. We children grew up loving our community and the people living in the community. As a child growing up, I was able to understand the impact a good environment can influence on a young child because, in our community, we, as young children, were disciplined by anybody within the community. Children were raised by the community. Mothers and Fathers look after their community's children, making sure they are doing the right thing, children played anywhere in the village and ate and drank water within the community's households, and sometimes mothers shared breastfeeding with another child, a mother breastfed the child for another mother in the community if that mother had gone to collect firewood or to retrieve water miles and miles away from home.

I was told by my Mom that she breastfed me up to the age of five because she wanted me to grow up a strong man to help my father in the garden and to help look after the cows and goats and sheep. I still remember how I was breastfed when I was old enough to be aware of it, and I remember so vividly the day my mother refused me not to breastfeed me. I was angry about it, and being young, I thought Mom didn't love me anymore because I was old enough to know what was going on. No matter how much my mother tried to explain to me why she stopped breastfeeding me, I was not convinced. All I wanted was breast milk because it kept me full and strong. I thought I had the right to continue to be breastfed by my mother because I had built a strong bond with my mother. I loved my mother so very much and she loved me back with all her heart, and she did all that she could to keep me healthy and strong and to grow into the healthy young men I became.

Mom did not want to see her son go hungry if we don't have enough to eat that night Mom would breastfeed me with the little breast milk she had, and I remember my father waking up in the middle of the night going to the kraal to milk a cow to come and feed me with when I was crying due to hunger at night. The milk will be fresh directly from the cow warm and ready for me to drink and fill my belly. These life experiences really made me grow up a very strong person who loved my parents every day, seeing my parents struggling to raise all of us and loving all twelve of us children unconditionally made my parents the best ones I would long for.

Growing up, we did not have much I had three pieces of clothing, one was my school uniform, the second was my church clothes, and the third was for playing at home and taking care of the animals. These clothes were always dirty and torn all over. I would consider them rags, not clothes, because they were all torn up. Sometimes I felt embarrassed wearing them, but at the same time, Mom and Dad had already made me aware that they couldn't afford to buy me new clothes because they did not have money. Besides, there were eight other children that they had to take care of. These experiences made me realize at an early age not to complain so much about what I can't afford but to be more appreciative of what I had and to give thanks to God for whatever I have and be appreciative and give thanks to God for what I don't have as well, but to be truthful, it was very painful as a child growing up not to be able to afford what other children had.

I always asked, "Why me?" when I saw my fellow kids having new clothes for Christmas, and I had to wear my old clothes for the big day, but my mother was always by our side doing her best to comfort their children, and I remember one day on Christmas eve, I returned home from visiting a friend of mine, a kid I always played with and on my visits. I saw the new clothes my friend had for the Christmas celebration his parents bought for him. He was very excited. He could not wait to show them to me, and he could not wait to put them on the next day to go to church with and play with other kids at church. I remember my friend asked me whether I too had new clothes for the Christmas celebration, and I remember telling my friend a very polite answer no. So that he didn't feel sorry for me, what I did I told him I don't have any, that my Mom and Dad are very poor, and they can't afford to buy me new clothes, but Mom and Dad were planning to kill the fattest animal for Christmas celebration so that we would be eating lots of food with my sisters and brothers, and I invited my friend join us and eat our food at our home since we will be having plenty of food.

As I look back as an adult now, it was a brilliant answer to my friend because I turned my friend's question from clothes to food, and I didn't want my friend to feel bad about me, but deep down in my heart, I was burning because on that Christmas day I would still be wearing my old clothes when my friends would be wearing their new clothes to celebrate Christmas.

I remember that day when I left my friend's home and went back home that evening, and I told my mother that my friend had new clothes for Christmas, and I asked my Mom if I could have new clothes for myself as well for the Christmas celebration that day. I remember how kind and loving my mother was to me having had my request for new clothes I could see in my mother's eyes the love she had for me. The first thing my mom said to me, "My son, I love you and I will always love you and your God loves you so very much and your God knows your heart and your feelings, and your God will not stop loving you because you don't have new clothes, but God loves everyone poor and the rich." As a child, I couldn't comprehend what my mother was trying to tell me, so I decided to do what children do best when they want something bad. I started crying, hoping that I would convince my parents to go and buy me new clothes.

When I started crying uncontrollably, my mom also became emotional. I could see the tears rolling down her cheeks quietly at the same time she was trying to console me. I remember I cried for several hours before my mom was able to get me to stop. After I had calmed down, my mother opened the granary, a small place they built to store food, and mother picked three small, ripe bananas and gave them to me to stop me from crying about new clothes. I remember my mother and I sat down, and she began to explain the reason why I didn't have new clothes for Christmas. She assured me that they were not refusing to buy me new clothes but simply could not afford to buy them, and that in the next year they would do their best to save the money from the sale of cotton and tomatoes and cabbages they grew for sale, and that assurance from Mom was so convincing, and I was so happy and grateful for my mom for that explanation and assurance.

Mom and Dad had open communication with us. They knew very well that open dialogue and communication will help them raise their twelve children with a lot of love and create peace in our house, and my father and mother never had formal education, but they had lots of common sense that helped them a lot in their decision making. My father had a seventh-grade education because his father could not afford to pay for his education my father told us how he wanted to further his education, but because his father was so poor and could not afford to pay the cost of education for his children. And being the firstborn of the family, my father was told to drop out of school and to help can help cultivate their large gardens so that they could harvest more food to feed the entire family.

During the family evening gatherings around the fire, our father always told us about how it was difficult growing up. Immediately after he dropped out of school to help his mother and father, his father fell and died due to a lack of medical attention. He did not receive medical care because there were no hospitals near their village to treat the sick people, so most illnesses were treated by witch doctors and traditional healers with locally prepared herbs. Most people in the community sought treatment from traditional healers, or witch doctors, as they are called, and most of those people who sought treatment from the witch doctors end up dying. Unfortunately, and my father told me that among those statistics of death in the hands of the traditional healers was his father and many of his sisters died at the hand of witch doctors treating them.

I remember my father telling me the story about his mother, and the pain she had to go through when she lost her children in the hands of witch doctors and traditional healers. She told a story of her mother taking her young infant child to a witch doctor because the child had a high temperature, and when her father and mother reached the traditional healer's home, the witch doctor took the baby in his hands and smeared the baby with the chicken blood for the diagnosis to find what was causing the child to have such a high temperature. and causing the sickness to the child and the healer diagnosed the child as being possessed by the bad spirits of his ancestors. So, to cure the child and remove the bad spirits from the baby, his father and mother should bring the fattest cow and the fattest chicken and a black sheep and a black goat, and the goat should be the fattest male goat because that is what the spirits demanded.

Father told me his mom and dad struggled to meet the demands of the witch doctor. They were told by the witch doctors that if they didn't meet those demands immediately, their child was going to die because the spirits were angry with them. My dad's father and mother were illiterate. They never attended school. Dad said when their father came back home to look for the fattest cow, fattest goat, fattest black chicken, and a black sheep and a black goat as the witch doctors demanded, it was the hardest thing his dad had to do but he had to do it to save the life of his child.

When all those demands were met, the witch doctor and the traditional healers were so happy because they knew they were getting a lot of food. The treatment began with the witch doctor taking the baby in his hand and cutting his body with a razor blade all over and the baby started bleeding uncontrollably, and the witch doctor smeared the baby with the traditional herbs he has made when the baby was crying because the pain from the medicine and the cuts.

The ritual was part of the cleansing to try to remove the bad spirits and bad omens from the baby and when the first process was over the witch doctors demanded the fattest chicken be slaughtered and the blood from the chicken to be brought to him to be given to the spirits and the rest of the chicken will be cooked, and only the witch doctor and no one else would eat the meat because it was the sacrifice to the spirits that was meant only for the witch doctor. The blood of the chicken was also smeared all over the baby's body as part of the cleansing.

According to my dad, the chicken slaughter was the first step of cleansing the baby from the spirits and bad omens. The second cleansing was to kill the black fattest goat, and the blood was given to the spirit and the goat meat cooked and shared with the witch doctor's helpers, and the last two demands, the fattest bull and the black sheep, were kept by the healer. My father said after all these rituals by the witch doctor failed to save the lives of his five sisters and brothers, who all died.

When my father was telling me this story about his mom and father, I was paying much attention because I didn't want to miss this very important history in my life what my grandparents had to go through to save the life of their children, and I remember asking my father why did the grandfather and grandmother take their children to the hospital instead of taking them to the witch doctor who hurt the children, and I remember my father telling me, "Son, back then there were no hospitals to take the sick people to seek medical treatment." And besides his people were illiterate with no formal education, and they believed the witch doctor would be able to cure their sick children. These traditional healers were the only place they could turn to seek medical help for their loved ones. The people in the community back then were treated by the witch doctors and traditional healers and both the traditional healers and witch doctors wielded a lot of power in the community and they were financially stable due to the food they were grabbing from the poor people in the form of animals, goats, sheep, goats, and hens by lying to the desperate people seeking a cure for their love ones.

The witch doctors are money-hungry people who fed on people's misery and desperation. They were manipulators who used tricks and deceit to get what they wanted from people. This story by my father cemented in my brain what I believed it was the right thing for me to do if I want to get out of poverty, and this story my father told me taught me how lack of education led their father to go to the witch doctor;

whereas, if they had formal education, they would have made a better decision for other alternatives to take their sick children elsewhere for medical treatment.

My father's story about his mother losing four of their siblings in the hands of the witch doctor affected me so very much as a child, and it reaffirmed to me the importance of me getting an education so that I would grow up well-informed and help my father and mother and my community. I wanted to make my father proud by getting an education, but the challenge I was facing was how I was going to do that was always in the back of my mind because I knew my father and my mother were very poor, and they would not be able to afford the cost of my education. At the same time, I knew my father and mother loved me so much that they would do everything in the best of their ability to make sure I do achieve my goals in life, and I knew at an early age that Dad and Mom wanted the best of me in life despite the fact that they were very poor.

CHAPTER 3:
My Father's Childhood and What He Overcame

FATHER TOLD US the story of how the death of his father affected him growing up. Since he was the firstborn in the family, he had to take up the mantle to care for the entire family, including his mother and stepmothers. His father practiced polygamy, and he had three wives. All the three wives had young children that he had to take care of at the same time. He had to defend their land from being grabbed by nearby clans who knew the head of their community, his father, was now dead.

Father told us the story about how he and his uncle and young brothers defended their territorial boundaries from land grabbers from a nearby clan. One day, my father said very early in the morning when he had just woken up and was getting ready to go to his garden when he saw a group of men coming to their community, armed with spears and bows, and he didn't know who these people were or what their motives were, but my father said that, because of his quick-thinking, he saved his community.

Father said when he saw these people, he knew something was wrong, so he blew a whistle made of a cow's horn to alert his community members that there was something wrong, because back then, the blowing of cow horn signaled danger and alerted the community. So, when he blew the horn, his uncle and brothers, neighbors, and friends came to help defend their community. When the attackers saw the large group of people that came together to help to defend their village, the attackers got scared because they saw that they were outnumbered, so they decided to retreat without attacking the community. The village was spared from losing their land that their father left for him and his brothers and sisters, and my father attributed that to his quick thinking and decision-making that helped him to defend their community as a young man.

My father was just fifteen when his father died and left all the responsibility to him. His father had cows, goat, and sheep, which needed to be grazed every day for grass and water, and he had to take that responsibility at younger age and played his role very well to help his mother and his stepbrothers who were left behind because of his Father's death. My father said that, as a young man, he became responsible for taking care of the animals—cows, goats, sheep, hens, and ducks to make sure all are protected from wild animals, like hyenas. This meant that he had to wake up at well before dawn to milk the cows for his mother, and then he had to take the bulls or oxen out of the kraal, and yolk them to prepare for plowing the garden with his mother to prepared it for planting crops, and this became his everyday routine for the rest of his life.

Father said his biggest challenge was taking cows and goats to graze for grass during the day because he had to travel ten miles or twenty kilometers in search of water for his animals during dry weather conditions, and when the animals had finished grazing and drinking water for the day and then he traveled that the same distance back home to bring the animals back in a kraal. At the end of the day, he was exhausted from the heat and the lack of help. My father said he had to do this every day because all his life and the life of siblings now depended on these animals and chicken and ducks that their father had left behind for them. When his mother saw how difficult and hard work his son was doing to take care of the family and the animals, her mother then decided to advise him to get married at early an age. According to his mother, marriage would help him overcome all the challenges before him, he and his new wife would be able to work together and achieved greatness in their life. My father's mother believed that it is only through marriage he would achieve happiness and be able to walk in the footsteps of his father and fill the gaps that his father left unfulfilled because he would have a wife to take care of him, and they would start to build a family together.

My father told me it was difficult to swallow what his mother was telling him because, at such a young age, he didn't know what to do. Besides, he did not have anything to support his wife, the only thing he had was a small grass thatch house he built with mud and spear grass, and he slept on the floor on a papyrus matt and one bedsheet. Thank God for providing the community with a warm climate so he need not worry about getting cold at night. My father said that his mother's suggestion that he get married was a difficult decision to make at such a young age, but at the end of the day, my father said a voice in his head told him that everything would be okay because he needed someone to be by his side to help him and support him of what he was going through.

At sixteen, my father got married to my mother through an arranged marriage. A family friend knew a girl in the nearby community, and his parents were well-known to the community, so the family friend, on my father's behalf, had reached out to the girl's family and asked the parents to allow him to marry their daughter. When the family friend told him that the parent of the girl had agreed to allow him to marry their daughter, he was excited about the news and his mother was also excited about the news because her son was going to get married, and she would soon be having a future daughter-in-law who would come and help his son and built a life together and raise children of their own. My father told us our mother was fifteen years old at the time of her marriage, so both were young, but they fell in love and they began to start their journey in life through marriage.

My mother did not have a formal education, either. She had second-grade education because her father refused to send her to school because she was a girl. Girls in those days were destined for marriage. Girls were viewed as a source of income to their father in the form of bride price that is paid by the groom's family. That her father decided to send only boys to school and left the girls out because he did not want the girls to attend school and the simple reasons for not sending girls to school is because it would delay parents from getting wealth in the form of a bride price paid to the parents of the girls once they get married to a man.

Unfortunately, girls in many communities around Uganda are still looked at as a source of wealth in poor communities because they are married to men at an early age and fathers demand many cows or cash in terms of bride price. My mother talked about how she begged her father to send her to school, but her quest for education fell on deaf ears by her father and that she cried with tears coming down her cheeks every day to be sent to school and get an education, but she was met with an angry father who sometimes beat her because of her quest to be sent to school, and her father considered her persistent asking him to be sent to school as being disrespectful to him, so she continued to face beating by her father.

Whenever our mother told us this story, she always wept. The little girl that yearned for education, but she was denied the opportunity by her own father—not simply because he could not pay for her education but because he wanted her to grow up and get married to a man so that he could get the bride price and cows from the marriage, and that was not good in the eyes of my mother, and everyone my mother told the story was touched by her story and couldn't believe why someone could do such a thing to ruin the life and the future of their own daughter. Her father denied her an opportunity to discover her talent and contribute to her community.

Even though my mother did not have a formal education, she was a person of high intellect and integrity. She knew the value and benefits of education and the impact of education and she knew what education could do for someone's life, and she became the champion of education in our house. She made sure my dad knew how important education was to a child's development especially to her own eight young girls. She did not want her girls to go through what she went through with her own father; she wanted all her girls to see inside the classroom and get an education, which would lead them to instill the value of education to their own children with their future husbands.

My mother also grew up in a polygamous community like my father, and my mother's father was a local chief in their community responsible for local tax collection, and he could send my mother to school, but because of his greed for material things and wealth as a tax collector he wanted more and more and refused to send our mother to school. Her father only valued boys, not girls, and he was able to send boys to school and let girls stay at home doing domestic work, like cooking for the family, cleaning the house, and fetching water for the family to use without attending school. According to my mother, their father wanted girls to stay home to wait for marriage. And, by staying at home, the girls would learn from their mother how to domestic chores such as keeping the house clean, learning how to cook for and take care of their husbands.

Being a local chief back then, there were privileges that came with the position. The local chiefs controlled the tax revenue collected by tax collectors, giving them authority over the local people in the community. He was able to marry many women and have many children. My mother told us her father had four women, and out of the four women, their mother was the last one her father married. None of the girls in those marriages went to school. All were left to prepare to get married themselves because of their father's greed for wealth from the cows that will be paid to him as a bride price during his daughters' marriage.

During the time when my father was growing up, the larger your family's size the more respect you received from the community. This is because you will have the manpower to use to plow the land and till the larger garden and produce large amounts of grains and food to feed your family and the village, as well. And, also, the larger family size was used as a means for security to protect and defend your territorial boundaries for your communities from other clans in the community.

The people within the community were producing many children because other children were expected to die due to diseases because of a lack of proper medical treatment for diseases in the community. Back then malaria, measles, smallpox, and sleeping sickness were the leading causes of death among young children, so to have a sense of security, mothers and fathers has to produced many children and hope and pray that some will grow and become an adult and help them and some will be taken away by the creator through deaths and my mother and father were among the lucky family in the community to be blessed with fourteen children, and out the fourteen children, two were taken away from my mother and father through death, but twelve survived.

Mother and Dad were a hard-working couple. They worked hard to raise their fourteen children of their own, plus the stepchildren left behind by their deceased father from the polygamous marriage. Growing up, Mom and Dad were our best friends. They both taught us the value of hard work and instilled in all of us the value that there is nothing in this world we could not achieve if we really worked hard for it. When I was four, Dad and I began to do things together. He began teaching me how to tie up the goats and sheep and how to collect all the chickens from around the yard to make sure they return safely to where they are kept safe to keep hyenas and stray wild cats from eating both the chickens and the sheep.

Dad taught me all the tricks of how goats can play with someone when they don't want to go and graze for grass but instead only want to destroy people's crops. From that lesson, I was able to learn from my dad the trick animals use to communicate with human beings and that lesson helped me a lot when I turned six years old, and my dad assigned me the responsibility of taking care of goats, sheep, calves, and birds. Early in the morning just before dawn., Dad woke me up. We went together to the kraal where the cows are kept separate the young calves from their mother to avoid them wandering with their mother and getting lost in the wilderness or left behind by the adult cows and to avoid them being eaten by wild animals. At six years old, another responsibility of mine was to make sure the cows were milked because it was from that milk that Dad and Mom earned their income to support their twelve children, so my role was to look after those young calves, and it was a very important role, because if I failed to do a good job then I would let my parents down, which, in my mind as a young child growing up, would have been a terrible thing to happen to me, since we all wanted to do our best in all what we do to help our parents the best we could. My parents instilled in me the value of hard work at a very young age, and I am proud of that and because of that, I was not afraid to face the world and be able to tackle any challenging situation that I encountered. I was able to determine to make a better life for myself and my parents, we were made aware that without working hard, we will not be able to have a better life, and that stuck in our brains as children and made us start to think differently as to how we would want to lead our life. My parents always taught us to do a great job no matter what kind of jobs we are doing we should do to the best of our ability.

All of us worked very hard to make sure we did not let our parents down, and that was the worst thing that could happen to us. We wanted to make our parents happy and be proud of all of us, since both our parents have shown all of us such great love despite the total abject poverty, they were living in. That did not stop them from guiding us and teaching has the simple truth of the value of a family. My parents knew the importance of family, and they knew that by having a family with strong family values they will be able to overcome all the challenges that were facing them. My sisters and brothers learned how to work hard from our parents by seeing them waking up very early at the wee hours of the night every day to go and till the land and prepare it for planting the crops and vegetables to support their families. Both my parents did this every day without complaining, and they knew it was the right thing to do to support their fourteen children. The hard work our parents undertook every day to support us made us all feel sorry for them and to take our role very seriously to make sure Dad and Mom were proud of us.

My parents had about fifty goats and about a hundred cows. All were kept in a big kraal made of heavy dry wood and thorns to prevent the animals from escaping at night to go and destroy people crops planted in the gardens and to prevent the hyenas from coming to eat the calves and the goats. Dad and Mom woke up at well before sunrise every day at night to go and milk the cow for sale and for us to drink in the early morning. My sisters and I drank fresh warm milk direct from the cow since we did not have electricity or fire to boil it in the morning so the only solution was to wait for the fresh warm milk that has just come out of the cow and the irony of drinking the fresh milk from the cow was to save us from being sick from the bacteria that may contaminate cold milk. Mom and dad's daily routine was to to milk the cows before dawn and yolk the bulls or the oxen to take them to the garden to till the soil in preparation for planting the crops.

All my sisters woke up before dawn to go and help Dad and Mom in the garden before they went to school. Coming back from the garden, we prepared to go to school tired without any breakfast or water to drink. The only thing that kept us going was the warm milk that Dad and Mom gave to us all to drink in the morning before we set up for school. This would have to keep us all for the rest of the day. My sisters and I had to walk ten miles to school every day, round trip. We had no shoes or school bag or good clothes to attend the school. At school, we are so hungry, with no food to eat and no water to drink. Sometimes, my sisters and I wanted to stop going to school, but we kept going because we did not want to let our parents down. Mom and Dad always had time to talk to us in the evening to encourage us never to give up. No matter how hard life is we should continue to carry on with our life with respect and dignity. Dad looked after the cows and goats during the day, Dad takes the animals to graze and look for water for the animals five to ten miles away every day, Dad came back home late at night very tired and exhausted but that did not stop our dad for being a dad to us. He made sure he talked to us all at night and asked us all how our day at school went and if we had enough to eat at home that night. Dad was a kind, compassionate, loving, caring father who every child would want as a father. He was kind and giving to all of us, and Dad would share any little food he had with all his twelve children. Dad had that gift of explaining things to us as to why we didn't have what other children have. He would call us all and sit us down every evening, if there is any matter, he wanted to communicate to us. In that process of communicating to us the issue of importance to our life and the life of our family, Dad would make us feel special despite our suffering from poverty. Dad would say we were reaching into our soul, and that made us see all the materialistic things in this world as less important to us.

Photo: My nephews plowing their land to prepare it for planting crops for food production for home consumption.

All my brothers and sisters were very close to one another and because of that strong value of love within our family we continued to love each other so dearly, protected each other in times of bad times, and be there for one another in bad times and good times and that made us build a strong bond between us all, and with that strong bond, we were able to achieve greatness in all what we did as a family. Our family earned the respect from the community because we had good manners and were respectful to others, we listened to our parents. Our parents taught us to listen to the teachers and be respectful to them because it's the teachers who will open the window of opportunities for our future, and our parents made sure we built a strong bond with our teachers in every class level we were attending, and we made sure we followed the advice from our parents.

All my sisters and brothers had very good reports from their teachers and every one of us had a good comment from our teacher about how well we behaved at school, and that made our parents so proud of us. The teachers would sometimes come to our home to tell our parent about how well we behaved at school compared to other school children, and our teachers thanked our parent for doing such a great job of raising twelve children with good manners and behavior, and that made both our parents so proud of us all, and we were proud of both of our parents to raise us to be respected by our teachers.

Mom and Dad grew vegetables, sweet potatoes, cabbages, cassava, yams, tomatoes, and sugar cane for sale to send us all to school, and it was our responsibility as children to help Dad and Mom in the garden because this was the only way our school fees get paid by Mom and Dad. They sold this produce to the local market to get money to pay for our school fees, we the children play a role in that every morning we wake up early before we go to school, and we go to the garden and help Dad and Mom transfer the young seedlings from the nursery beds to the gardens were, they will be planted and allowed to grow. It was a difficult job because it made us tired before we even got to school, knowing that we had to walk a distance to school without breakfast or anything to eat that morning if Dad and Mom don't give us the cow milk to drink before we can start our journey to school in the morning. That made it even worse because we would still be hungry on our way to school.

We knew early on that if we didn't work hard, we would not have any opportunities in life, but if we did work hard, we would achieve a better life because we knew education was the only way we can survive and change the trajectory of our lives and have better lives for ourselves and the lives of our children and hope to succeed and help our parents, as well, and that was Mom and Dad wished to see us have a better life, a life their parents were unable to give them—the chance to excel in school.

I remember one day on our way to school with my sisters we were so hungry in the morning and we did not have anything to eat. It was the month of April or May when mangos and other fruits begin to get ripe and ready for people to eat. My sisters and I decided to climb the mango tree to pick up the ripe mango fruit to eat so that we can have something in our bellies before we continued to school. The mango trees grow tall and picking the fruit requires someone to climb up high into the tree to get the mangos. With no support, the chances of falling to the ground are high, and that is exactly what happened to the younger Ajuk Ogwang. We climbed high into the mango tree, but, unfortunately, I missed a step and fell to the ground. Luckily, I wasn't badly hurt.

My sisters and I managed to get a few mangos to eat, and we proceeded to school.

Hunger hurts, and what hunger does to the child's body and mind is indescribable. It impairs a child's ability to concentrate on their work because they are hungry and their stomach hurts. I remember sitting in class one day, and I couldn't think straight, and my teacher saw me lying on the floor, and she came to pick me up and asked me what was wrong. I told her I was sick and that my stomach hurt, and I needed treatment, but the teacher didn't know that the only treatment I needed was food, and I was embarrassed to tell my teacher that I was hungry because I did want to be looked at as a weak kid among my classmates. Also, I understood that if I had told her that I was hungry, because the school didn't feed children, I knew the only thing she could do would be to send me home to my parents and hoping they could provide food so that I would feel better.

To make the matter even worse, it was the dry season which meant there was nothing to eat because all the fruits that children relied on were all dried up, due to the intense heat due, lack of rain, and the high temperatures of the dry season. I was courageous enough to ask my teacher to give me some clean drinking water, which would give me some strength to walk some distance back home to my parents, water itself was hard to find. The school had one borehole, which had to be shared with the entire community, so always it was packed with people looking to pump clean drinking water, and most of the time there was a struggle for water at the pump. People were always fighting at the pump, trying to get water, and that also affected my life as a young child growing up. I wanted to do something about that, and one of the reasons I wanted to get good education was with the hope that, one day, I would be able to provide clean drinking water in my community. Every day when I went to the pump to collect water for bathing and saw the number of families crowded in the same place looking to fetch water broke my heart.

For over 1 billion people, this is reality.

I remember when I was in the class when the teacher was conducting the lesson, I would not concentrate much or pay attention to what the teacher was telling the class. My mind would be thinking about what I could find to eat or drink after school. Hunger is a deadly disease to a child's development and concentration. I always wondered what I would have achieved in life if I had all the resources and nutrition food value required for the normal development of a child, and I will never know the answer to that question. My mother and father tried their best to provide for their family. They were deeply rooted in the family values, and they knew their responsibility as a parent to support their children, clothe them, feed them, protect them, and provide shelter to their family which they did that with whole their heart but their ability to provide more support was hindered by the evil in this world and that evil is called poverty.

Poverty is a dangerous thing in communities around the world, and I call all the government leaders, the civic leaders, priests, and all the humanity on this planet who care that all are created equal in God's image and that all children on this planet are entitled to have a better life in this beautiful world under the sun, that all children created in this world deserved to grow healthy and to be able to have enough food to eat to help them grow and all the children health and happiness is our responsibility and so all should do something about it and make poverty a thing of the past.

Every day, a child born anywhere on this planet deserves to grow healthy and be happy and no child around the world should go through what I went through growing up. I know that by coming together, we can do something to fight the evil of poverty and lack of food affecting billions of children around the world. When we come together as one person with one heart and mind with one common goal of fighting this evil called poverty and food problem around the world so that no child in any part of the world goes to bed hungry again. We should make sure that all children are given the opportunity to reach their full potential. No child should worry about where their next meal will be coming from, no mother should cry because she could not afford to feed their children. No father should be forced to sacrifice their food to their children and go to bed hungry because he wanted to make sure his daughter got enough food to feed them and be healthy like my father did to us, all the time sacrificing his food for us made for him by his beloved wife, my Mom for him to enjoy and be nourished to be able to steer the family in the right direction.

I lived it. I know the damage hunger can do to a child's mind. I am a living example of many children around the world, I always had that little voice calling in the back of my mind: "Do not turn your back to many children who are going to bed hungry around the world like you did when growing up in the rural part of Uganda Lira District." The little voice kept telling me, "Do not be silent. Use your voice." God has given you the opportunity to help children around the world. God has led you through to the promised land the land of the plenty, the land with plenty of milk and honey, the land of abundance, and it's now your turn to pay back of what the Lord has blessed you with, share it with millions of children around the world who do not know where their next meal is coming from, be that voice for that child in India, that child in Uganda, that child in Asia, that child in India, that child in the Caribbean, that child in Haiti, that child in Nigeria, that child in

Southern Sudan, that child in the Central African Republic, that child in Congo-Zaire, that child in Burma, that child in Rwanda, that child in Burundi, that child in Somali, that children in West Philadelphia, that child in Camden and that child in Ethiopia and that children in Palestine and the list goes on and on.

The whole world must unite to fight this evil called poverty and hunger around the world and the world must not continue to turn its back to this unthinkable tragedy where millions of children continue to suffer and living in poverty and some dying before their second birthday, the inhumane treatment of innocent soul must stop, and the innocent soul must have a voice in our midst. We must work together to provide to the innocent soul. I always wonder why God spared my life and why God brought me all that far thousands and thousands of miles away to a land in which I did not know anyone, a land that does not speak my language, a land with abundance, and I always ask, "Why me? Why me?" of the million people around the world then it was me who was chosen? It would be unwise not to think that the Lord kept his promise to my mother and father that I was the special child that I was born to the special parents. God wants me to fulfill the promised he made to my parents that this child born in a small grass thatch house built with mud-covered with cow dung would be the child that will be the voice for the voiceless children around the world.

CHAPTER 4:
A Childhood of Joy and Hunger

THERE ARE A lot of children in this world who go to bed hungry every day in Uganda where I grew up. I had a lot of family members and people within my community who were affected by hunger, who could not afford to feed their children the children go to bed hungry. To see the face of hunger in a child crying in the arms of their mother because there is nothing the mother can do to provide food to her child is beyond human comprehension, and I call on the the world to act and defeat hunger the entire world should come together and fight this war of hunger and defeat hunger and poverty for good so that no child can die because of hunger and malnutrition.

My sisters and my brothers were so lucky that we had parents who knew what a balanced diet could do for a child. Even with their lack of education, my parents knew how to plant various fruits, vegetables, beans, peas, oranges, mangoes, and to get milk from cows and goats. Mom and Dad made sure we ate a lot of vegetables and fruits as a child. Growing up, we thought our parents were punishing us by making us eat things that were good for us, or we thought our parents did not love us much because they could not provide us with meat by killing goats or cows.

Mom always prepared tomato soup, gravy mixed with peanut butter, and we ate it with sweet potatoes and at times my mother would prepare "boo," a green vegetable widely grown in Uganda. It's prepared by mixing it with sesame paste or peanut paste, and you can eat it with sweet potatoes or millet flour dough. Dad and Mom also grew a lot of cabbages for sale and that helped a lot to supplement our diet and keep our nutrition in check for all our sisters and brothers, so we grow up normal kids and healthy most of the time except during the dry season, which begins in November when all vegetables and fruits dry up due to extreme heat and sunshine. The plants and vegetables cannot withstand the heat and during this season. It is when the children of northern Uganda suffer a lot due to lack of food due to prolonged drought, and it is the hardest time of children in Lira District because you find most of the children are malnourished even the adults and their parents as well are so thin because this season food is hard to come by and very expensive to buy, and, with people so poor that they cannot afford to buy salt or a piece of soap, the poor children are the ones who suffer the most and a lot of them die due to malnourishment-related diseases.

As we grew up and became young adults and learned in school about the benefits of eating vegetables, we became so thankful to our parents for giving us the gift of healthy foods, which were freshly picked from our garden. They made us grow into strong healthy young men and women. And all of us felt blessed and thankful to our parents for allowing us to grow up in a family who loved us and cared for our well-being and health even though they were poor, and we thanked our parents for their common sense they had to raise us healthy even though they didn't have formal education to guide them or give them knowledge on how to raise their children.

Both our parents knew what kind of life they wanted to provide to their children: a healthy life. Mom and Dad wanted to provide food that will act as defense mechanism to protect their children from disease. They did not want their children to fall sick because they didn't have money or the means to take their children to the hospital or the health care center. Mom and Dad didn't have a formal education, but they did have the intelligence to decide what is best for their children and all the decision they make was always good for their children Dad and Mom had the common sense and that knowledge help them a lot.

They listened to each other's ideas and made decisions together as a family, and that quality led to many successful years of marriage.

I remember one day we were in a grass-thatch mud hut, sitting inside and resting with my father. At that moment, my father called on my mother to come in and have a discussion as to what they will do since the school year had begun, and they hardly had enough money to pay for the school fees for their children. My dad asked for advice from my mom about what they could do to resolve the issue. I remember looking at my mother's face and saw a mother with a lot of worry, despair, and helplessness. At first, she didn't have an answer for my Dad as to what they could do as a couple to resolve the issue of the school fees.

She continued to look at my father's eyes and she eventually responded by saying she would support any decision or suggestion my father would come up with to address the problem of the school fees. First, Dad told her he was contemplating selling the only big bull left in the kraal. Second, he was considering having all the girls stay at home for that school year term and having only boys go to school. The third option was to ask the school's administration to allow them to pay the school fees in installments. That would mean that the school would have to wait until the harvest period began because my mother and father had grown lots of vegetables, sweet potatoes, and cotton, so they had high expectation that the good enough yield would allow them to provide food for the family with enough left for sale, which will allow them to sell and get some money for education for all the children.

I remember my mother was not pleased with the second choice of making her girls to remain at home without going to school that term because that brought back the memories of her childhood, in which her father didn't pay for her education and only allowed the boys in her family to go to school, as she did not want to see that happening to her girls. For that reason, my mother explained to my father with conviction and passion what she thought of the idea of leaving the girls out of school, the effects that would have on the girls, and the general consequences that will be to the whole family. Through her logic, my mother was able to encourage and convince my father to go to school administration and explain that they had work hard that year and planted a lot of crops and vegetables for both home consumption and for sale, and that they expected they would be able to sell the excess harvest to raise some money to pay for the school fees for their children. So, both agreed, and Dad did as Mom has suggested.

My father went to the school administration to explain the family's situation and asked them to allow us to go to school without paying and that he will pay our school fees when the harvest period begins. Dad said it took her a long time to explain to the school administration because they did not believe that he would be able to pay for the school fees for his children, as he had explained, but Dad said after a long tough discussion and negotiation with the school authority the school administration agreed on that he could pay the school fees for his children by installment and that they were willing to allow him that duration of time he asked for and the length of time the school administration was to wait until when the harvest season began.

I remember Dad's returning home that day to convey the good news to my mother that the school had accepted to work with him on terms to allow all of his children to attend school on installment payments. Mom was filled with the joy that all her children would attend the school that term, and I remember Dad thanking Mom for her wise decision and encouraging him not to give up with the school administration. That day, Mom called all of us together and relayed the good news to us that all of us would attend the school that year we were all overwhelmed with joy of going to school. The girls were thrilled because they knew they were not going to have the opportunity since they knew that Dad did not have the money that year, so they thought their chances of going to school that year were zero.

Mom gathered us all together in the evening to talk to us and ask each of us how our day was. She always wanted to know how our day went. And, after laboring in the garden all day with my father, from four before sunrise until the afternoon, plowing and or tending to the crops in the garden, Mom always made sure we have something to eat in the evening.

And when Mom finished helping our Dad in the garden, her role turned to looking for firewood to cook food for us. She collected firewood from the nearby forest and piled it together and carried it on her head back home to cook for her children. Arriving back home, my mother then had to collect water for the family to drink and use for cooking and bathing. Mom's work was so hard which made us all children ashamed and be willing to help our mother at such a young age of ours we wanted to grow fast and help our mother. She walked five miles, carrying twenty liters of water on her head back and forth fetching water for the family to use at home, there was no nearby well or borehole water near or around our community, everybody in the community had to walk long distances to look for clean drinking water for their family to use.

After collecting water and filling all the water containers in the house, then my mother's attention turned to looking to what she could cook for her family that day. Mom's food preparation started by going to the garden and collecting some vegetables, sweet potatoes, or yams and coming back to peel the yams or sweet potatoes put them in a pot made of clay and cover them with banana leaves. Once that was done, Mom had to look for fire to start her firewood with lots of smoke especially during the wet seasons. It was very difficult to start a fire since all the firewood would be wet, and the grass used for lighting the firewood would also be wet.

These conditions made it difficult to start a simple fire, and we, as the children, sometimes could see the frustration in our mother's eyes when the fire failed to light. Mom and Dad did not have a place to store their firewood. All the firewood was piled under the house veranda or the granary shed, which was too small, and our grass thatch house was too small, with only enough room to keep food and to sleep. This meant that during the rainy season the firewood would be wet, but with that struggle, Mom made sure the food is prepared every evening for the family to eat. Once mom had prepared the food, she would gather all his twelve children together to come and eat as a family. Mom always made sure we were all present to eat together in the evening. When one was missing when the food was served, Mom made sure we all waited for them to come, and then we would eat.

What little food we had, we shared at these family gatherings, and this interaction built a strong family bond between us as brothers and sisters. We loved each other, everything we did in the house we did as a family. Dinner always took place around the big fireplace set up by our father who always made sure there were big logs of firewood to light the fire every evening. Once we finished eating the dinner, then it was time for our mother and father to talk to us and give us words of wisdom by taking time to pray to us and tell us to trust God and that the Lord would bless us from all our suffering.

Mom was a true believer in her almighty creator. She always told us, "Don't covet what belongs to others." As young children, we did not quite get what our mother meant by those words, but as I grew up, I thought about it, and I came to realize that Dad and Mom wanted to protect us from the worldly things so that we didn't worry so much about things we couldn't afford or want something that did not belong to us, that our mother was trying to make us feel better about ourselves, and that we should come to terms with our reality and know that we were born in a poor family.

Our evening fireplace gatherings were our favorite times because we got to spend time with our parents and hear stories from our father about their lives and the lives of their grandparents, and the community and war stories. These evening gatherings helped our family grow stronger and stronger every day because this was the chance both our parents encourage us to work harder and harder at school. Our parents told us we are special children and that we are the children of God sent to the world to do great things and that we will make the world a better place to live in by one day we will be able to help the sick the poor the hungry and that we will be given abundantly if we work hard for it.

Dad and Mom believed in hard work, they both know that the only way their family could come out of the vicious cycle of poverty was to work hard in all that we do and to instill in their children the value of work to their children and to encourage them to work hard to unearth their God-given potential talents. Mom and Dad knew that God has given each of us a talent, and it was our responsibility to discover those talents and utilize them to the best of our ability to benefit us and the community around us.

Mom and Dad always reminded us all to help and love our neighbor and to see every person around us as brother and sister and to always have that sense of community around us and because of that, we grew up all feeling loved by the people in our community. We were raised by a community of lovely people. We shared everything. I remember growing up that when my mother was unable to afford salt to add into the food that she prepared for his twelve children, she reached out to our neighbor to borrow some salt. Our neighbor gave her a spoonful of salt, and she came back and added that salt to the food she had prepared for her twelve children. As a young child, I was struck by how kind and generous this old lady was towards my mother because she was very poor as well, but she was kind and gracious to my mother, and she was willing to sacrifice the little that she had and felt happy that she was able to help my mother.

That moment stuck in my brain forever. As a young child growing up, I wanted to do things that could help people like what the elderly lady did to my mother to share the little salt that she had with my mother and feel so good about it that she was able to help my mother with salt. I wanted to be like her, and I wanted to go to school and have an education with the hope that one day, I would pay the old lady back with the act of kindness she had shown towards my mother by sharing her little salt with my mother. I will never forget that moment, and that moment shaped my adult life forever. I wanted to do things that will make a difference in people's lives in the community.

Mom and Dad instilled in their children the gift of love, respect, determination, self-discipline, hard work, and, above all, Mom and Dad instilled in all their children the love of God and that we should put God first in our life that in all that we do. God should be our guide and that our faith should always guide us all in our decision-making and that in all we do we should put God first. The love of God helped us so much. All twelve siblings growing up were God-fearing children. We knew that if we do something wrong, God would punish us and our parents, and we did not want that to happen to our parents who were the only people in our lives, and the only two people who could provide food for us, and we did not want to be among the massive statistic of orphaned children in our community who had lost their parents and were left at a young age to fend for themselves.

Growing up as young children, all twelve of us feared our parents dying. I remember one day evening we were all gathered around the fireplace listening to the story from our father and mother, and one of my sisters asked Mom and Dad, "What will happen to us if both of you die when we are still young?" It was a difficult question for a parent to answer, but at the same time, it showed my parents the fear, and anxiety we had about who would take care of us if they both died while we were still young, who would provide us with food, shelter, water, clothes all the basic needs that a child needs when growing up. My parents answered my sister's question with self-assurance that nothing would happen to them and that they would take care of all their twelve children until they become young adults and were able to take care of themselves.

My parents assured us that God would protect them from all the diseases of the world and that God will continue to provide my Mom and Dad with good health. Dad and Mom had a strong conviction on their faith they believed nothing will happen to them and that their God will help them out of all the bondage of suffering, and they were very optimistic for a brighter future for their children. Dad and Mom had set very high expectations for their children and they constantly reminded us that there is a brighter future ahead of us and that we should always work hard to reach on top of the mountain. And Mom and Dad always reminded us how we could reach the top of that high mountain and pursue all our dreams and the first lesson both Mom and Dad gave to their children every evening during those fireplace gatherings was that we should love ourselves, that we should love our brothers and sisters, and that we should show love to everyone and, above all, to love our God.

We all grew up loved by many in our village. We never disrespected anybody in our community, and we treated everybody the same, whether or young or old. My mother and father constantly reminded all twelve of us children that the key to success in life is to have respect for everyone and that respect should begin with you, and by you respecting yourself and being humble and having compassion in your heart and they assured us that if we do all that, people would respect us back. As a young man growing up, I couldn't comprehend what my parents were trying to communicate to us, but as I grew older, then I began to see exactly the lesson I learned from my uneducated parents played out to my real world, and I began to thank them every day for instilling such a very important lesson in my mind at such a young age, and because of their lessons, I was able to take the right path in my life and thank my Mom and Dad for that I will always be grateful for their lessons to me, and I will continue to teach the same lesson to my children.

Dad and Mom, even though neither had a formal education, both were very smart. They had a routine they drew up for us all twelve siblings to follow. One routine was that each evening everyone gathered around fireplace prepared by our father was the time that our father and mother would listen to each of our concerns and try to help us through that difficult time and encourage us all to be our best in all what we are doing and to encourage us all on how we can overcome our challenges facing us. Also, the fireplace was used as a place for Dad and Mom to communicate to us regarding the matter of school fees, since we were twelve siblings attending primary, and school fees were always a problem.

Sometimes, some of my sisters are left out of the school calendar because my parents could not afford to pay for their tuition fees. Mom and Dad had ten girls, but two died and eight lived. Mom wanted all her eight girls to attend school so they would have opportunities in life to become strong women and help our community. Mom did not want to deny her girls the opportunity to attend school as her father did to her. She wanted the best for her girls, but that was not going to be easy since my parents had no way to pay school tuitions for all the eight girls and four boys, but my parents were determined to make sure all the eight girls to attend school. Mom and Dad worked very hard each year to grow up vegetables and sweet potatoes for both for sale and consumption. The excess sweet potatoes and cabbages were sold to the local market to raise funds to pay school fees for their twelve children. Sometimes, the money was not enough to pay the school fees for all of us, so Dad had to plead with the school to allow the girls attend the school without paying when the school fees were due but to work out a payment plan with the school administration to allow him to pay the school fees by installment until he was able to complete the balance for the tuition for all of us. Sometimes the school agreed with the arrangement. Sometimes they did not, and if the school fail to agree with the arrangement, that means that year the girls would be left home without attending school. They would have to wait for the next academic calendar year after my parents had saved some money. Then they will all be let go back to school again the next academic year.

I remember one day my next oldest sister did very well with her school grades, and she was admitted to secondary school. She was very excited that she was going to attend secondary school, but her excitement turned to tears. I remember her loud crying after our father told her she would not be attending secondary school because they did not have the money to pay for her tuition. My sister cried for days without eating. She wanted to get a secondary education, but her dream was crushed since Dad and Mom could not afford to pay for her tuition the school was demanding.

My sisters were devastated by the news because they all knew that none of them would have the opportunity to attend secondary school or college. Mom and Dad one evening gathered us all around the fireplace to communicate to us what the future held for the girls. The fireplace gathering was a place dedicated to us all when our parents want to give us life lessons in life, telling us family past and present stories that would change our lives and encourage us to work harder to achieve whatever goal we want to achieve, or the place where we would get lessons from our parents that would help us all in our quest to obtain greatness and success in all what we were doing to have a better life than our parents had.

Dad always made sure he had enough firewood to produce enough light for us to see us all our faces and tell us all how beautiful and handsome we were to them, and Dad and Mom always made us feel special. Mom has always made us know that God has created twelve of us because he had a plan for each of us and that if we continued to pray to him, we would be able to achieve all that we need in life. As for our mother, she instilled in us the fear of God and the love of Christ, and that made us all forget about our poverty since we knew there was somebody above us all looking down upon us, and taking care of us and listening to our prayers and our dreams, every one of us asking him for a better life for us and our parents and that we are here in this world for a purpose and that purpose was to do good in the eyes of God and continue to help one another and be human to all by doing things in our community that are pleasing to the eyes of God by being there for one another in times of needs and to serve other people with respect and dignity.

I congratulate our parents for giving us the knowledge and sense of knowing that there was someone above us all. We knew what we are going through in life and our suffering, I remember that even if when we go to sleep hungry, we all woke up with no anger toward our parents. Instead, we continued to love them more and more that is the time we built a bond between us as siblings and built strong love among us that grew stronger and stronger. We, the children, never complained to our Dad or Mom why we cannot have what other children had because we love our parents and our parents has made us all know we were a very poor family, and we accepted the fact that Dad and Mom were poor so we would have to work together as a family to help our parent to be able to raise the twelve of us. The evening fire gathering every day was viewed by our parents as a time for both spiritual bonding and family bonding among siblings and the method worked well for us all we all grew up with strong family love and Mom and Dad offer us all support. I gave thanks to our parents for such a strong lesson on family values we grew up with even though they did not have the formal education, but they set us a high standard and high expectation for their children to follow, which would later help us all in our daily life experiences and to help us instill the same family value and life experiences to the life of our children, and I am so grateful that they did that to us all.

CHAPTER 5:
A Mother and Her Daughters Fight for an Education

THE DAY WHEN Dad and Mom had planned to communicate the message to the girls about the future of their education, Mom first came quietly and lay her goatskin mat near the fireplace close to the girls and sat down quietly and did not mention a word to the girls like she normally does, but instead she came quietly and sat down on her skin goatskin mat, and we knew straight away there was something wrong because Mom always was the happiest person around the fireplace and was always taking the lead in all the conversation around the fireplace. That day was the darkest and the saddest in our mother's life. We all were saddened to see our mother sad and helpless. Mother had big dreams for her girls, and she wanted them to have the best education they could, the education that her parents did not give to her the opportunity to go to school, and now the same was happening to her children due to poverty.

After Mom came and sat down quietly on a goatskin mat near the firewood, Dad followed her with his stool made of think mahogany wood and, for a moment, when Dad sat on his chair there was silence. We children did not know what was going on, but we were eager to hear what Dad was about to communicate to us all; instead, Mom began by saying a prayer and continue to say how both loved us all. No matter what happened, we had a bond that tied us together till eternity we were one family with one body, and we will be a family forever and ever and that made us feel good. As a family and as children, we knew Dad and Mom were going to be there for us forever, and it was comforting to hear such a message from our parents and that gave us a sense of peace and comfort in our minds as children. After Mom had finished praying and giving us all a blessing, we continued to observe the silence waiting for what Dad was about to communicate to us all, when Mom had finished praying and saying a word of comfort, peace, and support, then it was the time for Dad to come in and start is part to communicate what he needed to tell us all, but his message was directly to the girls, and the news was they were going to be unable to come up with enough money to continue to send the girls to further their education and that the girls would remain at home after graduation from seventh grade to help at home and wait to get married, and then their husbands would take care of them, and that only boys will continue to go to school because boys have a better chance of obtaining a good education and helping the family.

The news was so devastating to the girls that the others started to beg Dad and Mom to give them a chance to continue with their education. Mom began to cry, as well, and before long, all of us were crying around the fireplace, including our father. Mom and Dad became helpless and so emotional to see the tears in the eyes of their girls they did not know what to do. That evening of the fireplace was the worst day of our family history, the day that my sisters' futures became dark and never brightened again. It's the day we will never, ever forget. It's the day the life and dreams and hopes for my sisters were blown away in the wind and never to return. Mom held her eight daughters close to her heart and cried together with them. I remember the pain my mother was having at that moment and days and months and years to come never stop. It brought back all the memory to Mom of her plight in which her father denied her education and forced her to get married at such a young age, she didn't expect the same thing to be happening to her girls.

Mom wanted to go to school and get an education and change the lives of girls around her community and herself, but her father failed her, and when she spoke to us about how she wanted to go to school so badly but her father could not allow that to happen, Mom said that was also her darkest moment in life. Mom now was faced with this dilemma again and now this time her children, I remember our mother saying to us, "No mother should see the pain in her child's eye and be unable to take away that pain from their children." It was painful for both my parents as well as all the family. Our parents' dreams were to see their children growing up happy and becoming young adults and becoming successful and giving back to the community.

Mom felt she had let her daughters down, and she wished there was anything she could do to help her daughters at that moment, but there wasn't. She had to look at all options available out there to help her eight girls, but there was nothing that could change the situation, because the issue was the money that could help save her girls to go back to school, and they did not have that capability of coming up with that money. Mom always said to us every evening that if her father had allowed her to go to school and she obtained the formal education, she was going to make sure we were taken care of and not face the problem we were going through at that time because she was going to make sure we had a good education and obtained a good job to take care of our children in the future.

When Mom held her daughters for several hours and comforted them and consoled them as what mothers do best because Mom felt there is nothing she could do but to stay strong for her daughters and to encourage her daughters to continue to work hard and support themselves and continue to advise her daughters that the struggle continued with them to fight for girls' education wherever life would take them in terms of marriage, meaning that Mom new the only good thing she can do is to help her daughters understand that any man that her daughter would meet and want to marry them must put the education of girls first in their mind and that the husband of her girls will treat the girls' education the same as those of the boys.

Mom knew she had a long fight ahead of her for girls' education, Mom became an advocate for the girls' education in our community by talking to other parents in our community about how important is to send girls to attend school and gain knowledge and become strong independent women. At that time, girls' education was seen as a waste of time or that delayed the family from getting the bride price paid for them when the girl gets married. It's a tradition practiced among many tribes in Uganda. Girls back then got married at the early age of twelve, and most communities in northern Uganda practiced arranged marriages. This is where a family acquaintance of your mother or who had a daughter or a son arranges for those two kids to get married, even if the boy or the girls don't love each other, as the girls are forced to marry the man they don't even know and verse versa. The family in the community has turned to marriage as a source of wealth because the more girls you have, the more cows or money will be paid to you because each girl will bring a different number of cows to the family, depending on how wealthy the family of the groom is. The more wealth the groom's family has, the more demand the bride's family will make.

The marriage of the bride is not complete until the number of cows demanded by the bride's family is agreed upon. The bride's family may demand a certain amount of money, a certain number of cows, a certain number of large saucepans, or clothes for the bride's mother and coats for the bride's parents. If all these demands are not met by the groom's family, the bride's family will not allow the bride to leave with her future husband. My mother's message was not received well by many parents in our village because they saw her as trying to change the clan and community culture of the family she was met with resistance by many families. As a child, I stood close to my mother listening to her talk to other families about education for girls. I did not quite get it or understand at that time why she spoke passionately about the education of girls, but as I grew up, I started to understand why my mother was so passionate about girls' education.

I knew that Mom wanted the best for her girls and for all the girls in her community. After Dad communicated to the girls that they will no longer be going to school to further their education. They cried and cried, but nothing could be done that tears in my sisters' eyes gave them a blessing. God saw their grief and pain, and they were given the strength to move on in life. They began dedicating their life helping our mother in their garden. After their seventh-grade education, one by one, they began to drop out of school because Dad could not afford to pay for their education. Each day, my sisters woke up early and went to the garden with my mom. They tended the garden until it was time to come home to prepare the meal and then they were off to the bush to look after the cows until sunset. My sisters travel five to ten miles every day to look after the animals and take them to drink water and bring them back to the wooden kraal to protect the animals from being eaten by wild animals like hyenas.

This became the daily routine for my sisters helping my father and mother in the garden and helping my father with the animals at home. My sisters were hard-working girls and God-fearing girls. Their love of Christ and the fear of God gave them the strength to move on regardless of the hard times they were facing. The love of Christ opened their eyes and gave them the innermost peace and made them believe everything would be okay. They also received continued support from our Mother, and that unconditional love gave them the courage to move on no matter what. My sisters were very strong women with sound minds and intellect with the seventh-grade education. Dad and Mom gave to them they were able to make good decisions for themselves and because of their sound judgment my sisters were loved by many in our community, and all were accorded respect.

My sisters became a symbol of respect for the community, everyone in the community admired my sisters the way they conducted themselves. They set a high standard for the girls in the community to follow, they had manners and class and respected for all, whether they were old, young, elderly, blind, or mentally impaired. They didn't discriminate and made our father and mother proud. I remember there were two men in our community one had mental health challenges that needed care and walked naked. The other was affected by leprosy and was deformed in both his hands and legs. His ears and nose were deformed, and could not speak well, and he could not handle food well, and no one loved this man because they thought if they associated with him, his curse would come to them or if they associated with him, they would catch his disease.

My mother welcomed these two men in our home with open hands and gave them food and water every day, and I remember Dad giving one guy the only trousers he had left because he saw the man walking naked with no clothes on. Dad felt it was the right thing to do to give this guy his trousers. Every morning, this man showed up in our little hut, sit under our grass thatch house, and wait until my father and sisters came back from the garden and prepare something to eat to share with these guys. I still remember vividly their names. The mentally challenged man who walked around naked was called Kali, and the one with leprosy was Orech. My sisters never looked down upon these two gentlemen. They never treated them differently than others they knew it was the Christian way to do good to others regardless of their economic status, whether you are rich, the sick, the poor, and the mentally challenged, and that was the way our parents taught us. It was humbling to see the way my sisters treated these two gentlemen whom society had already judged and condemned, but not my sisters. They welcomed them with open arms and made them feel welcome.

Ours was a home where everyone was loved, fed, and cared for, a home with kind hearts, a home with compassion, a home in which they are provided with shelter and clothed. All of these acts demonstrate the simple way Christians should lead their lives, and I saw it at the heart of my eight sisters' lives. A life must be about service to others. When you begin to think that I think I am blessed with plenty, and I need to bless someone else's life by caring, feeding the homeless, caring for the sick, clothing the naked, and being there for someone who need your support, being a voice of encouragement to others not to give up no matter how hard life has become. Let that person know things will be okay and be there for someone who is thinking the world has turned against them let them know things will be alright. Let that person believe that things would turn around and he or she would be able to lead their life to their God-given potential. When you do all these things, your life will be fulfilled, and you will have a happy and a joyful life. My sisters' lives were full of joy, compassion, happiness, and above all, they put God first in all they were doing. They all decided to put God first. All my eight sisters became a shining light and beacon of hope in the community and a voice for the voiceless children in our community and the community around us.

Every girl in our community wanted to be like my sisters, every parent in our community wanted their girls to copy the good examples from my sisters. My sisters didn't chase after boys. Instead, they spent most of their time helping Mom and Dad in the gardens and taking care of the animals, after Dad could not afford to pay for their education. My sister tells the story of one day when they took the one hundred cows to graze for grass and look for water almost ten miles away from home. They were young girls with little food to eat or water to drink. My sisters said during the day, it became very hot with temperatures over 100 degrees Fahrenheit. They become dehydrated because of lack of water and no food to eat, they became very hungry, and they wanted something to eat to give them the strength and to keep looking after the cows and to make the journey back home.

So, my sister said they hatched a plan to look for wild fruits growing in the wilderness so they could have something to eat in the process of looking for the wild fruit, they lost contact with where the cows were grazing, so they could not locate the cows, and this was so devastating for the girls. First, they did not know what to do. Second, they did not know what Dad would do to them. And third, they worried that the livestock would be stolen by thieves.

Because they were so young, my sisters said they started crying because they did not know what else to do. They did not want to cause another problem for Mom and Dad on top of the problems they already had, so my sisters said they had to start looking for the lost animals all night, and the fear that they would be eaten by wild animals terrified them. At the same time, they did not want to go back home without the cows, thinking that will be the worst thing that they could do to their parents. So, they had to stay out all night in the wilderness, looking for the lost cows, goats, and sheep. As my sisters tell the story, both of them slept in the bush that night. When they awoke, they continued looking for the animals, not realizing the pain and suffering they had created for their parents because both my mother and the other brothers and sisters thought that lions or Hyenas must have killed my sisters and ate them so my parents had to set out that night looking for them in the wilderness.

Thank God for providing a bright moon and stars at night in Africa that helped the searchers the vision to see at night, the quiet and peaceful night with the birds singing, and the hyenas and lions roaring for hunger from different angles. At night, it was a very tough thing to swallow but according to my sisters they had to stay strong knowing that their God of Abraham and Jacob would keep them safe, so they continued throughout the night looking for the lost cows and sheep and goats. Unfortunately, they could not locate the animals, because at night the animals also found a place to crowd together and sleep. The girls hoped to find a cave in the anthills and hide themselves to provide them with shelter and warmth until the daybreak very early in the morning then they will begin their search for their animals.

At the same time, my Dad and Mom and other young siblings also went looking for my sisters in the wilderness, but no one knew what direction they took so the only to do was to pray to God that the Lord will guide them to the right direction to look for where they were, so, the family all spread out that night looking for my lost two sisters in the wilderness. Nobody from my family slept that night. We were determined to find the two sisters and bring them back home safe and then we would become one family again. Being a young boy, I was told by my parent to remain at home because I could not travel such a long distance, and traveling through the thick bushes and sharp thorns was hard to manage because we have to walk barefoot in the wilderness, without shoes on, and if you are not strong enough, you come back home with wounds and sharp objects in your feet, but I wanted to join my siblings to search for my beloved two sisters lost in the wilderness.

I felt angry that I could not do much to help my parents and my siblings even if I was still young and could not do much. At the same time, Mom and Dad had instilled in me that it was the man's responsibility to take care of women and that included my sisters, and, at that moment, I wanted to show to Dad and Mom that I cared, and I wanted to go out and look out for my sisters. I felt helpless and I felt I have let my parents down because I can't help them at that young age. My mother and father and other sisters and other older brother continued their search for my two sisters all night, but they could not find the whereabouts of my two sisters, the process continued until daybreak.

Mom and Dad were full of fear that the wild animals might have attacked my two sisters and killed them. At the same time, they had full confidence in themselves that the girls were safe, and they would find them alive again. Dad and Mom had a strong faith in all that they did, and their work was guided by faith, so they believed in their hearts that their two daughters were safe, and that they would look for them until they found them. When the daylight broke that morning, and the red sunlight of Africa spread across the land. This is the time when the animals woke up and were hungry and wanted to start eating the grass when is still cold with dew on it to provide them with water. It was also the time when the mother of a young calf wants to feed their young ones, so they make a braying sound to wake the young ones up, and it is a good time to track where the mother cow is bellowing for their young ones. The sounds of the cows guided my parents to where the cows are, and they hoped that they will also find our lost sisters with the cows together and bring them back home safely.

Mom and Dad continued to search for my two sisters all day and finally, they made a breakthrough when they located some of the animals. The rest were scattered all over the place, and Dad and Mom knew they were close to locating my lost two sisters along with them. My two lost sisters also woke up very early and very hungry and dehydrated with no food or water for two days. They were weak and couldn't walk long distances, so they kept walking slowly while looking for the lost livestock. Dad and Mom had a whistle made of cow horn, which was used for alerting the community when there was danger or any serious matter affecting the community that needed to be addressed. The whistle is blown to alert the community members, but Dad also taught us that in case when we got lost in the wilderness, he would use the whistle to locate us. So, when we heard him blow that whistle, we should walk towards where the sound, and he would be able to find us. So, my sisters knew the sounds of the cow horn.

The cow horn flute did not sound very far but had a deep sound for us all to hear. So, when my two lost sisters heard Dad's blowing the whistle, they knew it was Dad looking for them, and they followed the sound until they reached Dad. When he and Mom saw their lost two daughters, they ran towards them and hugged them and there was a sigh of relief that they were alive and safe.

They were weak but strong girls. Neither of my sisters complained to Dad as to why he and Mom sent them to the wilderness to look after the cows at that young age. They knew it was the right thing to do to help Mom and Dad. They had to help Dad and Mom because if they didn't, there was nobody who was going to do that and help Mom and Dad. Once my sisters were located and found alive, it was time for Mom and Dad to turn their attention to locating the lost cows and sheep one by one until all were found and returned to the kraal for safety.

Mom and Dad worked so hard that day to make sure all the animals were accounted for and that all were gathered and taken to the kraal and Mom and Dad was able to gather all the animals including the goats and sheep and brought them back to the Kraal where all of the animals are kept. During the time my two sisters were lost in the wilderness, the entire family was saddened by the events, but we young ones did not know what to do. We knew we wanted our sisters to come back home safe and sound, and we continued to pray together as Dad and Mom taught us that when there is a problem we should pray to God and that God would send his angel to help and protect us so when this happened this was a big test of our faith for us all young children left at home.

For me and my siblings who were left behind, we wanted to test the truth of what Mom and Dad taught us whether God will grant us our wishes. We wanted to test what Mom had taught us at at a young age and that was to pray and asked God for help in all our trials, and for this particular time, we were praying for God to help bring back our two sisters lost in the wilderness safe back home. We prayed all night. We could not sleep alone in the grass thatch hut, fearing someone was going to come and attack us, since Dad and Mom were in the wilderness looking for our lost two sisters. This was the first test of our faith as children to learn that when we ask something from God with pure intent, then God will provide to us. That very night we, the young ones left behind, prayed and prayed to God to please bring our sisters back home safe and bring Mom and Dad back home safe as well so that they come back home and Mom to cook for us food because we were so hungry since there was nothing to eat at home or nobody to cook for us and when the evening came.

When we saw Mom and Dad walking back home along with our two sisters, we were full of joy and excitement, and we believed that God heard our prayers and brought back our sisters, and to have Mom and Dad safely back home was further testament from Mom and Dad that God heard our prayers, and that God would provide to us all what we need as long as we worked hard and asked God with pure intent. My sisters were my role models even though they went through a difficult challenge of growing up in a poverty-stricken household which prevented them from continuing their education. They never blamed Mom or Dad with all that they were going through because they knew in their heart that if Dad and Mom had the financial means of supporting them, they would not have hesitated to provide the support to all of their eight girls, so they knew Mom and Dad had no means or resources to support their eight girls, and, therefore, they didn't complain but instead they continued to work hard collectively to help Mom and Dad in the garden and looking after the cows, goats, and sheep to support the family.

Even though my sisters grew up in total poverty, they never gave up hope that one day things would be better. They were full of dreams and high hopes for themselves and a better future for their children. All my sisters had compassionate hearts to help everybody around them and everyone in our community loved them back. Because of their kind hearts, they help anyone in need of help without asking for any kind of payback they knew God would one day pay them back as our mother and father taught us the principle of giving back to your village and the reward and the blessing you receive back by giving back to the people in need in the community.

Despite growing up in a very poor home with nothing to eat, no running water, no electricity or candlelight to illuminate the grass thatch house, or fancy clothes to put on, they still had hope for a better future for all of them. All my eight sisters were able to listen and learn from Mom and Dad and became the best girls and best mothers to their children. Poverty is the deadliest disease that must be fought at all costs. The world must unite together to raise this issue of poverty on an international level so that people will work together to fight this evil called poverty in the community around us and bring children born in poverty to have access to education, health care, clean water food, or clothing so that children around the world from poor countries around the world will be able to compete with other children from well to do countries and by doing so, they would benefit these poor children to dust off and maximize their God-given talents to the fullest, and in turn, help others in need. No one or child should be asked to be born in poverty-stricken home, but we find ourselves in a home God gave to our parents, the society must fight this evil so-called poverty with determination and zeal.

I know and witnessed poverty first hand in our home and the community around us, and I know what poverty can do to someone mind especially as a child growing up it can affect your growth if you are not strong enough to fight this evil called poverty, many innocent precious lives will continue to get lost in the dark and the world can do better by changing the trajectory of poverty in the community we live and the best medicine to change the trajectory of poverty in our community is education and what my sisters went through gave me a lifelong lesson. While growing up, I wanted to see what I could do to help the young girls and boys growing up in poverty in my community and in my district and other parts of the world so that they didn't go through what my sisters went through in life, in which poverty denied them the chance to attend their basic right to education to maximize their God-given potentials. My sisters were motivated, smart, intelligent girls. If it weren't because of the poverty that denied my sisters their basic right to education.

I still strongly believe if my sisters were given the chance like many other children around the world born in a poverty-stricken community, they would have been a force to make the world a better place for all to achieve their God-given potential. When all my sisters were unable to go to school because my parents could not afford to pay for them to continue with their education, I saw the pain in my sisters' eyes, the pain I could not take away from them because the only treatment for their pain was to provide to them the money to pay for their education, but because of our poverty, our mother and father could not provide the treatment to my sisters. Their quest and yearning for education affected my life forever as a young boy growing up among eight girls. My mind always thinking that when I grew up I would make sure all girls attend school beginning from my community and going elsewhere around the world. These dreams have resonated with me all my adult life.

My sisters had that instant love for one another, like my mother had, and they were not materialistic women. They led simple and quiet lives, but what they did spoke a million words to the people around them and the people they came across. Most importantly, they set a good example to follow for the young girls in our community. They were the light of our family. Mom and Dad were proud of their accomplishment of raising strong and independent girls. Despite the fact they were poor, with a seventh-grade education, they made sure that they could not be stopped from making a difference in the community they lived in, and it was a good lesson to all the people in our community that you need not be rich or have PhD to make a difference in the world, as long as you stay focused and open your mind to think broadly in terms of what you want to achieve in your lifetime, nothing will stop you from obtaining your dream. Even if it takes years to achieve the dream, never give up. Even though there is a rough road to your dream, which sometimes knock you down. Do not let that fall deter you from getting up and dusting yourself off and beginning to walk the narrow path again.

That fall should even motivate you to even work harder than you have ever done before, sometimes the path to success is achieved by falling many times, but the key that is when you fall will you be able to accept your responsibility for what led you to fall to the ground and learn that lesson and get up stronger than before. Life is full of challenges and temptation, which we as human beings should accept and be willing to work on the challenges before us and avoid the temptation of an easy, quick fix to our problems, which can lead us to do things that are not pleasing in the eyes of God or the people around us. Achieving your goals is not done in one day or one night.

One must have a long-term goal in that one should be able to operate within those set goals, as a young boy growing up in the rural place in Adwila village in the Lira district of Uganda, I saw the suffering of my mother, father, and sisters. I watched my mother cry because she could not raise money for school fees for her daughters. I watched her cry because she could not afford clean clothes to go to social gatherings. I watched her cry because she did not have food to feed her children. I watched her cry because she couldn't afford to take her children to the doctor for treatment because she didn't have the money. I watched her cry because she could not afford to provide us with a clean bed or something to sleep on. We all slept on goatskin mats, which provided warmth to us at night, no bedsheet to cover ourselves at night, but with all these problems surrounding my mother never let these problems deter her from providing the best advice as a mother can give to her children and to show to us all the children that unconditional love to all of us and giving us all the hopes to believe in that everything will be okay.

CHAPTER 6:
The Yearly Battle to Pay Tuition

~~~~~

G ROWING UP IN poverty helped me see the world from a different perspective. The one thing I knew for sure was I did not want my children to go through what I went through. I wanted to get out of poverty but growing up in a country where the life and future of children from poor families are so dark, meaning that if your parents are so poor there is no hope for you to get out of that poverty because the only way out of poverty is to have an education, but education is not free in Uganda. It is expensive in Uganda, and if your parents are as poor as my mother and father, then you would remain in the cycle of poverty for the rest of your life because your parents can't afford to pay for your education.

I knew I had to work exceptionally hard to achieve my goals if I was going to come out of poverty and have a better life for me and my children. At the young age of ten years old, I began to plow my garden with Dad's help and plant cassava yams, and when they were ready for harvest, I uprooted them carry them on my head to the local market for sale, and the little money I earned from that sale of the cassavas helped me buy my clothes and the balance of the money I gave to Dad to help him pay for my education. During those days, Mom and Dad were growing cotton in a large field, and as children, it was our responsibility to weed the plants, and, during harvest seasons, to gather picked cotton in 50-kilogram sacks and carry them on our head and bring them back home for sorting and prepare them for sale into the market to earn Dad and Mom some income to help to provide the school fees and buys clothes and school uniforms for their twelve children.

The cotton plantation was very labor-intensive. First, Dad and Mom woke us all the children before dawn every day and we would yolk the animals and take them to plow the garden. Sometimes, we stayed in the garden until late afternoon. Working every day in the garden without food and water was a very challenging task for children to endure. But, at the same time, we did not want to let our parents down by refusing to help them. We sometimes become so hungry and thirsty, since we were working without anything to eat or drink. Our survival was dependent on eating fruit from wild plants, mangoes, wild bananas, wild guava fruits, and oranges. These were our best bet to get some immediate relief for our hungry stomachs.

At that early age, I had already laid all my plans out in my mind, and the goal I wanted to achieve in life—and one I continued to work hard every day—was to help my parents as best I could so that they would be able to provide to me and the younger siblings and to respect my parents because they were the key for my success in life, and the second goal was to make sure I attended school every day even if I was facing challenges, including going to school hungry and sometimes not having enough money to buy me a book to write, walking barefoot on the hot sands of Africa, but because I knew education was my only best hope to get out of poverty so all these challenges were part of the goals I needed to overcome to get where I wanted to be in life. The third goal I made for myself was to make sure I was well behaved at school and listened to my teachers and ask them questions about the areas I don't understand, and another goal I made for myself was to make sure I associated myself with kids who had the same aspirations for a better future.

These were long-term ambitious goals, and I knew it would take me a long time to get to where I wanted, and I knew it would take a long time and hard work to achieve the goals. Another long-term goal I set for myself was to build a better house for my parents to live in when

I finished my education and find a good job to support myself and my children, and the last goal I made for myself was to support my beloved parents who had sacrificed so much to raise all the twelve children and loving them all unconditionally for the rest of their time on earth. It was a big goal and a big dream, but I knew I could do it one step at a time and with the help of our parents supporting me along the way through and encouraging me all the way through and them letting me know that I was loved no matter what happened was a powerful voice to a young man growing up, knowing that every time I did not achieve my expectation, there was somebody there to say it was okay to fail in certain areas. At the same time, they were very clear to me by saying to me that I should not let those failures stop me from pursuing my goals. Despite having only having a seventh-grade education, my father was able to articulate very clearly to me that failure and success go hand in hand and that I should never allow failure to stop me from pursuing my goals and dreams. As a young man, I quite didn't understand what my father meant by those words, but as I grew up, I started to understand what my father meant. I came face to face with obstacles in my life that I thought I was not going to overcome and move forward with my education.

One of the obstacles that could have stopped me from achieving my goals was peer pressure. At the age of twelve, boys were dropping out of my school to get married because their parents wanted them to get married and have children to go and help in the family farm fields because they saw education as a waste of time for their children. Because education was very expensive, most parents at that time wanted their children to get married at a young age so that they cannot have the burden of paying the school fees.

I was mocked by many classmates who had dropped out that I was wasting time getting a Western education. As I walked to school or during the social gatherings, I was teased, and I can remember when we had heated discussions as to what benefit would I get by staying in school when there is no guarantee that I would find a job, and they would try to persuade me to drop out of school and join them, get married, and have children, I remember asking my peers, "How could you have children when you don't even have a house to live in, clothes to dress the child or even the clothes for you and your wife to wear?" That didn't make sense to me, and because of that I didn't want to see my children going through what I was going through, and my peers didn't know that it was one of my goals set never to see my children suffering again. It was tough to overcome the challenge, but I was able to overcome it and move on to the next level in my life.

Another reason why parents were forcing their young men to get married was because of the cattle rustlers the primitive tribe called the Karamojong tribes that lived and occupied the eastern part of Uganda were stealing cattle from the Langi tribe, and they were killing many people in the Lango region of Lira district in Northern Uganda where I lived with my parents. The Karamojong tribe practiced a nomadic way of life. They were pastoral people who moved from place to place with their families and animals in search of water and grass for their cattle because their land is semi-arid desert with little grass for their animals to eat. The men of the Karamojong tribe seek to marry who own wives a lot of cows, which meant that if you're not rich with cows, then your son would not get married, so what the Karamojong men did was to train their young men to become warriors at an early age ready for them to raid nearby villages to loot goods, which included food cows, goats, and sheep to take to their parents.

This barbaric process was viewed by many in the Karamojong elders as a way of initiation of young men into adulthood. The more cows young adult men brought to the Karamojong community or their family, the more respect one would command from the elders of the tribe within their community. The Karamojong cattle rustling was the biggest challenge that affected the Langi tribe for a long time and affected the livelihood of the Langi community since most of the wealth for the tribe was in their cows.

The Langi tribe used their cows to sell and send their children to school. the cows are used for plowing to prepare the gardens to plant crops for family consumption. Cow's milk was used by many Langi tribes to generate income by selling milk to the local market to buy essential products like soap, salt, sugar, and food. When the cows were taken away from our people, there was no way the affected families could afford to pay for the education for their children. As a result, many children within the Langi community had to drop out of school. While in the act of cattle rustling, the Karamojong warriors killed a lot of people within the Lira district and the neighboring district of Lira. The Soroti and Gulu were the most affected, and among those statistics, the warriors killed my nephew who was left to rot on the ground. Because most people had fled the villages in fear of their lives, there was nobody to bury him. He was just twenty-five years old.

The death of my nephew affected my sister mentally and emotionally. She did not know what to do because she feared for her life and the life of the remaining children, and she could not return to her home knowing that the Karamojong warrior would come back again and killed her and the rest of the family, so my sister had to remain in hiding in the bush for a long time with her children and wait until the Karamojong warrior returned to their district, and then they returned to their village to bury her son. The Karamojong warrior terrorized the three districts of Lira, Gulu, and Soroti in Uganda for a long time without the government's intervention to help the local people.

I remember my father and my mother waking us up in the middle of the night telling us we should go and hide in the bush because the Karamojong warriors were coming and that they were killing people they found in their way. It was in the middle of the night, and it was raining and dark since we do not have electricity in our village. As a child, it was difficult waking up in the middle of the night when it was very dark, and you do not know where. You were going not only afraid of the darkness but the fear that you may find wild animals that would attack you and eat you up or the fear that you will be attacked by dangerous and sometimes poisonous snakes, like cobras or pythons that were very common when I was growing up, and pythons had attacked people and eaten many cows in my area. I remember my mom and dad struggling to wake us all up.

We didn't want to go in the bush that night, but they told us that it was a matter of life and death, that whoever didn't want to go to the bush that night should brace for death because the Karamojong would come and kill them. It was a difficult decision for my parents, as well, seeing your children with no good clothes on that will give them warmth, seeing your children feeling cold, and you have nothing like warm clothes to give them to keep them warm, and my parents couldn't start a fire at night to keep the children warm with the fear that the smoke and the fire would lead the Karamojong warriors to them and kill all the children, so they didn't want to take that chance, and I remember my mom holding us in her arms like a hen or a bird protecting her chicks from danger, but my Mom wanted to give us warmth, and when I think about it today that memory alone gives me chills, and it showed me how wonderful our mother was to us all, and how she loved us all.

Mom and Dad were the most beloved parents any child would want. I remember my little sister started to cry in the middle of the night in the bush where we were hiding, and Mom was whispering to my little sister's ear to quiet down. I could hear that quiet tender voice coming from my mother, the voice of love that only the mother can have to saw love to her child and keep her child calm and make her child stop crying. There were lots of mosquitoes in the bush, and we all were wet and cold with mosquito bites all over our bodies. We didn't have a choice but to run and hide with our parents for the fear that if the Karamojong warriors came and attacked our village, they wouldn't find us.

What the Karamojong warriors did when they found an empty house empty was to set it on fire and burn it to the ground. If they find people inside the house find the house, they killed all the occupants of the house and burned the house down. Sometimes they burned the house down with the people inside the house, killing everyone. Karamojong warriors torched many of the grass thatch houses for people in our community and many lost their animals to the Karamojong warriors, and many families were left homeless without food to eat since the granary used for the local community for food storage were burned down by the warriors. And when this happened the community are left with nothing to eat, and starvation became rampant because people's houses and food had been destroyed by the Karamojong warriors.

The Langi livelihood depended on agriculture and farming and rearing animals, but since all these means had either been destroyed or taken away from them by the Karamojong warriors, the result was poverty and starvation. Many families begin to let their young boys and girls get married at an early age because of the fear that their animals will be taken away and their sons would be left without cows to pay for the bride price for marriage.

I remember my father telling me he wanted to have a talk with me, and I was wondering why my father wanted to talk with me, and I kept thinking maybe I did something wrong, which was not pleasing in the eyes of my father, and he would talk to me about it and advise me to correct the wrong. It was in the early evening after he had just returned from grazing the animals and taken the animals in their kraal to sleep for the night.

Dad had a little stool he sat on it is made of local timber, and he made it himself. Dad loved to sit on that stool every day. He came back from the garden, grazing animals, or any trip outside our home when he came back home, he asked us to bring to him that stool to sit on, so we already knew when we see our father coming back home from his outings to make sure his stool was ready for him to sit on in the spot where he always loved to sit. The stool was his favorite chair to sit on, and we all respected that chair so very much no one sat on that stool unless Dad asked us to, and we all realized that when Dad wanted to communicate a very important serious message to us, he used the stool, so it became a very important chair in our family. So, that day when Dad came back from grazing the animals, and he asked me to come and sit down near him because he wanted to talk to me, I was very much concerned about what Dad wanted to talk to me about.

When my father asked me to come and sit down on the ground next to him, he was sitting on his stool my thoughts ran from being scared I'd done something wrong to thinking maybe my Dad wanted to tell me to help look after the cows the next day because he may be traveling somewhere. But all the thoughts I had turned out not to be true. The real reason why my father wanted to talk to me was about marriage. Dad wanted me to get married at twelve years old.

This request was born out of the fear that the Karamojong would come and take away our cows, and Dad wanted to protect his young boy by letting me have a wife at an earlier age. Dad sat me down, and I remember sitting next to my father motionless, listening to my father talk about the decision he wanted to take and the reason as to why he made the decision that I should get married at such an early age. I still don't know what my father expected me to say to him about marriage as a young boy of twelve, but I remember I responded to my Dad's request as a young person would respond by saying to him that I was still very young to get married and that if the Karamojong came and wanted to take away the animals let them take cows because I know I would be okay.

Having told my dad that I was still too young to get married, he didn't continue to force the issue. My father understood very well where I was coming from, that I wanted to continue with my education, and I was determined to do it at any cost without anything getting in my way. When Dad knew there was nothing that he could do to convince me to get married, he turned to his secret weapon. That secret weapon was my mother, but what Dad didn't know was that Mom and I had already had that discussion about marriage even before my meeting with him, and I told Mom that there was nothing that would come between me and my education, and I let Mom know my determination to get an education no matter what happened to our cows. Even if the Karamojong came and take away the cows, I was still going to get my education. At that age, I didn't understand the ways and means by which I was going to pay for my education if our cows were taken away.

It was a challenging thought knowing that the only resources you had might soon be taken away, and I will not be able to go to school or have a meal or a balanced diet which the cow's milk provides to the growing child. But, in the back of my mind, it was very tough on me as a young boy, imagining all our of cows being taken away, our sole livelihood, and we would be left in the dark with nothing to take care of our brothers and sisters. The idea that the cows and goats and sheep we all depend upon would no longer be there was a scary thought as a young boy. I didn't know where to turn to for help and advice since my parents were also having sleepless nights that all their animals, which were their livelihood, would be taken away.

As a young boy, I was aware that we were a poor family, and I was aware we could not afford much to feed all of us, knowing that the little that we had was being taken away from us. It's not something a young child growing up should have to go through. It is a terrifying feeling, going to bed wondering whether you will be killed at night by warriors, wondering whether you will have something to feed your stomach for the day. The Karamojong war affected the Langi so much that every community was left with no education for their children because most of the schools within the region were closed for the fear that the Karamojong warriors would come and attack the school and kill the children. Their parents also refused to send their children to school because of the fear that their children for the same reasons.

There was food insecurity in all of northern Uganda since animals that helped families to plow the land had already been taken by the Karamojong warriors. With food insecurity in the region in which there was starvation and rampant malnutrition in the region. Children were dying of preventable diseases like malaria, diarrhea, and malnutrition. The food planted in their gardens was all destroyed by the Karamojong warriors. Huts and granaries were burned to the ground. Huts sometimes were torched when people are sleeping inside and granaries used for food storage were burned, leaving families with nothing to eat, since their survival for the rest of the seasons depends on the storage food to take them to the next planting season when families will be ready to plant new crops to prepare for the next year. The family supermarket for a Ugandan village in those days was their granary since there were no stores back then, and even if there were supermarkets, families were so poor to afford to buy food since they do not have money or income at all to buy even things like soap and salt.

The damage that the cattle rustlers did to the people of northern Uganda was long-lasting. Generations and generations to come will pay for it since the big vacuum was created when no children were going to school, and the schools were mostly closed during those years leaving Northern Uganda with a gap that would take a long road to recover from in quality of income and education. Now, there is an imbalance in terms of education level, income, and development compared to other cities in western Uganda, and this drop in quality was due to Karamojong cattle rustling war that affected northern Uganda for many years.

The northern part of Uganda was left undeveloped compared to the other regions in Uganda who had relative peace throughout the years. There was income inequality as a result of the prolonged war that affected the northern Ugandan people in relation to in other regions of Uganda where people earned more money than those in northern Uganda due to the education gap that was created as result of too many wars that affected northern Uganda. This created a big gap in education because many students in northern were not reaching the higher institutions of learning many were dropping out of college at an early stage either because many of their parents could not afford to pay for their education because their only resources were cows and sheep and goats that had been taken away from them.

The lack of development in the northern part of Uganda, as compared to the regions with relative peace throughout the years, was due to a lack of security. The people of the Northern part of Uganda were left with no choice other than to run to save their lives, leaving them unable to develop their communities, since development comes when there is peace. The education standard dropped to below the required standard because the schools weren't open during the time of insecurity and the teachers were operating under constant fear of being attack by the Karamojong warriors, as a result, performance in both colleges high school and the secondary level dropped.

Parents were in constant fear of their children being abducted by the Karamojong warriors and killed and because of that constant fear convinced parents not to send their children to school to learn, and the result was there was high illiteracy in the northernmost part of northern Uganda compared to the other region of Uganda where security was good, and those areas were peaceful. The effect of the Karamojong war had created a big gap in terms of employment balance in the country since the education in the northern part of Uganda has been affected so much during the insecurity that fewer people graduated from college from northern Uganda and as a result that region was left behind compared to other regions in the country because they couldn't compete with other brothers and sisters from other regions who had a relative peace in their region and had better education and this led to more government office was being filled by the people from other regions of Uganda since they had the qualifications and education needed to do the work, and the northern people were left behind since their education standards could not meet the required standard and the result was an imbalance in development as well.

The destruction of schools in northern Uganda by the Karamojong warriors led to the stagnation of the education progress in the area since the community felt the government do not care about their people. When the government failed to provide adequate security in a timely manner to save their citizens from the brutality of the Karamojong warriors. As a result, many communities did not care about education anymore. They saw education as a waste of time since their government was not even doing enough to try to save their lives and the lives of their children from the brutality of the Karamojong warriors. The Karamojong war lasted for a long time before the government began the disarmament of the Karamojong warriors. For twenty years, northern Uganda lived at the hands of this Karamojong terror with little or no effort by the Ugandan government to intervene and help the northern Ugandan people regain their peace and stability. Northern Uganda was once a source of the Ugandan pride in terms of their education system, their wealth in cattle ranching, and a cooperative society that was formed in the community to help the poor people. The cooperative system provided the means to buy produce from the local people like cotton and tobacco, giving families the needed money to send their children to school. All that was destroyed during the war and has never recovered.

Northern Ugandans were known for their strength and critical thinking, especially the Langi and Acholi tribes. Both are Luo-speaking people. The president that brought Uganda to independence from the British rule was from the northern part of Uganda, and he was of the

Luo-speaking people in the Langi tribe. His name was Dr. Milton Obote. As a young man, I was so proud of my country for having gained our independence from the British government rule. Obote worked so hard to free Uganda from British rule and bring democracy into Uganda. Growing up as a young child, I remember how the community was involved in the local election to select their leaders and how celebrant the people became when the party they were supporting won the election. When October 9, Ugandan Independence Day, came every year, there was celebration and jubilation within the community and the celebration goes on for many days in the community people drinking and eating lots of food. In our community, it was celebrated using community drum beating and big bull and or cow or goat was killed on that day for the community to feast on, and there was lots of local brew made of sorghum and millet and the entertainment was provided by the local village people, in which people sang our local Langi songs and danced to the tune of our traditional dance. It was a reminder of me of how rich our culture was, seeing women and men dance to our traditional music was an amazing thing to see as a young child, women shaking their behinds or buttocks to the beat of the local drums, and men jumping up and down, dancing to the local drums was entertaining and an amazing thing to see.

The community was full of joy and excitement and they had high hopes for their children, and I remember my mother and father telling me that the sky was the limit for me. Opportunities were wide open for me since we were now in a free country. The Obote government brought high hopes for the community in Uganda during the time Uganda got her independence from the British, and the young people were eager to pursue their dreams, and we were all full of hope for a better future since most people knew that we had a democratic government by which most people would be judged first on their ability to perform the job, not on the color of their skin or the region they belong to or where they come from or the tribe they belong to or the language they speak. We all were to become one Uganda.

We were proud of our country, and I still am. Uganda is a beautiful country and was considered the pearl of Africa by the British colonizers because of its beauty endowed with natural beauty and sunshine and its wet and dry seasons were perfectly aligned. During president Obote's regime, young people became so much involved in politics every tribe in Uganda had the opportunity to express their opinion whichever way they could. Schools were lively, young and old were involved in the democratic processes, both on the local level and in the government without fear of being intimidated whichever way. As a young child, I was attracted to politics. I saw it as being a cool thing to do, and I wanted to be a politician when I grew up.

I saw it as a neat job to do where one's role would be going to the community and talking to people and try to solve people's problems. I saw politics as means to how I would design programs to help the community I lived in. I was motivated to politic as a young child to learn from the people around me and gain as much knowledge as possible to better the life of my community. I asked Mom and Dad several question about politics and what it meant to be independent, and I remember asking my father, "Does it mean we are not independent now?" As I grew up, I wanted to gain knowledge to help my poor parents, so I decided to try to learn from people as much I could to gain knowledge to better my life and the life of my family, and I decided to learn and I was prepared and committed to educate myself as much as possible, and I was ready if it would take to get to my goal of achieving my education goal. I was willing to continue to go nonstop until I reach that required goal. I knew at a young age that I did not have any influential person that will help me with my dream, neither did I had any good mentors to look after apart from my father and my mother who were everything to us.

My brain stayed focused on one thing and that was to stay at school and get an education and be able to complete in the world and be able to improve the lives of my family and lives of people within my community, so I knew early in life that in order to achieve my dream I would need to work extra hard because I came from a poor background and poor family with no name recognition and it was up to me to build that good name for myself and for my family and the community I live in. And I knew at an early age that whatever good thing you do to your community to help other people you will be noticed and appreciated, and people will give thanks to you, and you will be praised, and they will give you the support for the development for a better future. You will be given a platform to reach out to different people and absorbed as much knowledge as you can and to build my network as much I could and be known to the community so that they would know who I am and who my parents are.

I wonder now where that motivation and determination came from when I was still very young, but what I do know I credited that to my parents for giving me that determination by making me feel worthy and them believing that I can do anything I want in life even if I came from a poor family background, and I also credited my father and mom for setting for me high expectations and standards to follow. Father and Mother were loved in their community they were pillars to their people. They put God first in all they did. Dad planted lots of tomatoes and cabbages in our shared gardens and during the dry season. People from the village would come to our home asking for tomatoes and cabbages to feed their children because they will have nothing to eat and feed their children.

From the month of October, November, December, January, and February the northern part of Uganda experiences its annual dry season. Temperatures rise well over 100 degrees, and at those temperatures, all the crops and trees dry up due to the lack of rain. The only way people could grow vegetables to eat was when they have a wetland nearby. Dad and Mom farmed a wetland near our home where both of them could dig and prepare to plant crops on it and use the water to traditionally irrigate their crops to avoid the plants getting dried up. My mom and dad were so lucky to have had this wetland near our home to turn it to good use to grow crops during dry seasons to feed us and feed the community around us. The main crops that Dad and Mom were growing in our wetland were green vegetables, locally known as "boo" in our local language of the Luo language and other crops dad were growing in the wetland was the tomatoes and cabbages. These two cops require lots of attention, so we, as young children, played a role in helping Dad and Mom. We watered the plants very early in the morning before school and in the evening after school. This becomes our daily routine for the rest of the season to make sure the plant does not dry up due to extreme heat. It's hard work for the young child but because we were all trained to help Mom and Dad.

None of us ever complained to Dad and Mom that the work was difficult. We saw it as a way to survive. If we didn't contribute to help Dad and Mom, then we would all suffer, as other families were suffering because they were starving. We worked as a team, and we all loved each other. Mom and Dad managed to teach us that no matter how hard and difficult life was, if we all worked together and help each other, we will be able to overcome the challenges we encountered. Dad and Mom taught us the value of hard work, and we all became hard-working people. We followed what Dad and Mom told us. We listened to their advice and their teaching, and we made sure we took it into our hearts, especially the message of putting God first in all that we did. We all believed that we would not be able to succeed without putting God first. Dad and Mom became the people we looked after.

They became successful parents because raising twelve children in such extreme poverty was not easy. It takes dedicated and committed parents to do that, and Mom and Dad were truly heroes to their own twelve children and heroes in our community. They were loved by the community we lived in and outside the village. They become the voice for the voiceless for us all and the people within our community and neighboring community. Mom and Dad laid a strong foundation for all their twelve children. They were the best role models every child would want from a parent. As a child, my mother and father was what I called the first line of defense, meaning that they are number one that children learn the good values that will help them grow up as a responsible adult.

No one should doubt their ability to do great things. No matter your economic and financial status, you can still make a great contribution to this beautiful world. Parents, let your presence be known to your children. Let your children see how great you are by your positive contribution to the community you live in. Let your children see the positive role model you are to their life, fear not to tell the truth to your children, fear not to have straight forward and candid discussion on a difficult subject with your children, by doing that you are teaching them the value that life is not easy but with hard work, they can achieve anything they want in life.

Be that Mom and Dad whose door is always open to your children whenever they need your advice. Be that parent who knows every challenge your children are going through and be able to welcome them with an open hand and said to your son or daughter that everything will be all right. Be that parent who is always talking to your children and encouraging them that all the time that they can succeed and not let them give up. No matter how hard it is, they should continue to push on. Be that parent that you pour all your heart to love and protect and support your children emotionally, spiritually, and economically if you can but above all give them love and support this will show to your children that you care about them. What I learned from my parents, I learned that they were on top of their game by paying attention to what the children were doing, and they were the first ones to support us in whatever we decided to pursue. Whatever a child chooses what she or he wants to do in life, please do not discourage any ideas that she or he may have in mind and want to do. Just be there and support them with all your heart and might and whatever resources you may have to support them, but just by being there for that child and encourage that child is all that child need and to let him or her know that she can do whatever they can do with hard work and determination.

Dad and Mom were perfectly good examples of good parenting in our community. With no formal education of their own but they were full of the knowledge of how they wanted to raise us all. Dad and Mom continued to be our guide and mentor and someone we look after in times of need and in tough times.

CHAPTER 7:
Growing up as a child during a dictator rule Idi Amin Dada

I AND MY SISTERS and brothers had very big dreams when we were growing up, the Obote government inspired children because they wanted to be part of the democratic process during that time. Children at my age during that time had dreams of becoming lawyers, doctors, politician, and teachers because of the inspiration they saw from the people in leadership, and they wanted to be part of the democratic process since Uganda was still a young democratic country having just won their independence from the British rule.

President Obote, as I remember, was not a military man, but he was a smart democratic president, and he was willing to work with anybody regardless of religious background or tribe, and people from all walks of life in Uganda loved him, and the Ugandan economy at that time was growing at a fast rate. There was less corruption in government. Schools and hospitals were built in all districts to address the health care needs of the community. As I remember, and the Ugandan people were so proud to be in a country that prided itself in love of country, and the pride for the government that cared for his people since the government was for the people and by the people.

As a young child, I remember Dad and Mom carry their cotton on their head to sell it to a cooperative society or unions to earn money to buy essential goods for their family. At that same time, that was happening all over the country, and life for the poor was going on well because families can afford to buy salt and soap, sugar, books, and uniforms and pay school fees for their children. All in all, the economy was thriving and growing fast. The Obote government was full of bright and intelligent men and women who were fully dedicated to civil servant duty, and they perform their duty to the best of their ability to serve their people but, unfortunately, the army and the defense department was occupied by the people of low level of education, and, for that reason, there was no disciple in the army among the military.

The young men and women in the military were not taking seriously the human rights of the Ugandan people and as a result, a lot of innocent people lost their lives during that time. Human rights violations were at their peak among law enforcement. I remember as a child growing up, I was scared to see a man in an army uniform and carrying a gun because I was told by people in my community that a man in uniform and carrying a gun would kill me. So, as a child growing up in the villages, we were told by our parents that when we saw a person wearing a military uniform, we should run as fast as we could and hide away from them because if we don't run away, the man in the military uniform will likely kill us.

The situation became so bad as I remember as a young child, we were not allowed to travel to the nearby town to buy things because of the fear that we will be killed by the military, and as a young child, I always wondered why this happened to children or why men and women were killed for no reason or why someone would kill for no apparent reason. I did not have an answer to such question, but I was curious that one day when I grew up I wanted to know why that had to happen to innocent people who had done nothing wrong, and I wanted one day the government in power to tell me why they failed to protect their people from the army when their role to me was to protect their citizens from harm's way, but instead they turn on to kill their very own, the people they are supposed to protect. The situation became worst when Obote's army chief of staff overthrew his government and declared himself the president of Uganda. This man's name was Dictator Idi Amin Dada. He was a real dictator. When he took over the government from Obote by coup, I remember as a young child growing up a lot of people were killed, both people working in the government, government leaders, and government heads, and civilians. This guy killed indiscriminately, and people were scared to death, including our parents.

They did not know what to do. the Uganda future became dark, this dictator Idi Amin Dada killed the most prominent people in government, including our beloved Bishop from northern Uganda. Bishop Jonan Luwum was looked to as a man of God by young and old people alike. As a young child, I remember thinking it seemed the world was coming to an end because, if this man, dictator Idi Amin Dada, can kill a holy man a man of God doing God's work, we young people in Uganda were scared to death, and no one knew what the future held for the people of Uganda.

The poor people turned to God for an answer as they always have and asked God for protection because they knew nothing is impossible to God. All people from all religious walks of life turn to pray to their God. As a child, I had never seen that strong unification in people's faith with one common purpose to ask God to help people in their community and for the protection of its citizens from this evil man dictator Idi Amin Dada.

People started asking themselves if this man can kill the innocent man, a man of faith the bishop Jonan Luwum doing God's work, then who are we for this madman to spare our lives. People became afraid to go to church because the rumors were circulating that Amin Dada had ordered that anybody found gathering in the house of worship be killed. The killing of Archbishop Luwum brought fear and sorrow to all Ugandans, especially the people living in Northern Uganda because people did not know what the dictator Idi Amin Dada was going to do next. The poor communities in Uganda were full of sadness and despair because no one knew where to turn because their Archbishop has been murdered and their faith has been put to test, whether their God was alive and well. If he was, why had their living God allowed this Dictator Idi Amin to take the life of their beloved Archbishop Jonan Luwum?

As a child growing up in the rural part of Uganda, I remember having many questions in my mind and questioning the existence of God because of many atrocities being committed by this dictator Idi Amin Dada. As a child, I remember turning to my mother and asking why God has allowed this evil to happen to the people of Uganda and asking my mother whether we could kneel and pray to our God and to ask God for forgiveness of any wrong we have done to him and ask him to forgive the people of Uganda and save the Uganda people from this evil man causing suffering and pain in heart of many Ugandan families and the communities across Uganda children were scared as well as adults.

Amin's soliders began killing people for no apparent reason. Bodies of innocent people were all over town with no one to bury them because of the fear that Amin's soldier would find people and kill them. Dictator Idi Amin Dada had also ordered that women wearing miniskirts must be burned alive. Any woman found wearing a miniskirt must be killed, women became traumatized and scared by the news, and women did not know what to do. Amin's soldiers began to implement the order, so any women found wearing a dress that was shorter or above her knee was either raped or beaten, and a lot of women lost their lives as a result.

Also, Dictator Idi Amin Dada ordered that no one could wear flip-flops on the street across Uganda, and if you are caught breaking the law, you were beaten or sometimes even killed. There were stories that Amin's soldiers even made people eat their flip-flops once they were caught wearing them on the streets. There were no human rights in Uganda. Life was a nightmare for all Ugandans of every background—the old, the young, the elderly, Christian, or religious organizations except for the Muslim faith were the only religious faith organizations spared by the dictator Idi Amin Dada because he hailed from the Muslim faith. Idi Amin tried to divide us Ugandans from our freedom of worship. We, as Ugandan people, had that privilege of religious freedom, whether we were Christian, Muslim, Judaism, Buddhism, or other religious denominations, we had the privilege of practicing our faith according to our traditions without any interference from the government authority, but the Idi Amin Dada regime wanted to divide us by our faith and tried to make other religious denomination less important than his Muslim faith. He wanted to divide Ugandans based on their religious belief something many Ugandan rejected that notion because Ugandan had coexisted for many years with many religious faiths, and many Ugandan saw coexisting with other religious dominations were our strength because we could learn from each other's faith and support each other with the common goal of seeing each other as the children of God created in God's image.

During Amin Dada rule all the Uganda were scared to death, there was no hope of a better life, every smart Ugandan was being killed there was no rule of law except to follow Dictator Idi Amin Dada orders. As a young child, I began to think if there was any meaning of staying alive or even going to school because there was no point to go to school since everyone was being killed, parents stopped sending their children to school, there was no social gatherings at school or in homes because of the fear that Amin's soldiers would come and kill everyone because they thought any public gathering was a plot to overthrow Idi Amin Dictatorial government.

Amin killed a lot of the Langi and Acholi people. Both tribes were the Luo-speaking people and the tribe to which the former president Dr. Milton Obote belonged. When Dictator Idi Amin overthrew the democratically elected president Obote by coup his goals turned to Langi people to make sure all the people in leadership were either captured and put in jail or killed, I remember as a young child in our community each and every day we learn that somebody within our district has disappeared and cannot be found and traced whereabouts and then after some time, people will learn that that person was found killed and dumped in the bush or sometimes the body was never recovered. Amin's soldiers killed a lot of the Langi tribe. Sometimes, the bodies were found in town rotten with no one knowing where the dead body came from. Some bodies were brought by Amin's soldiers after they'd been killed far away and were dumped in the Lira district.

This put everyone in fear of their lives. Whenever a loved one disappeared, you will look for them because if you were caught doing that you would also be killed.

There was a girl from our area, and she became one of Amin's several women that he had. One day, I was walking to go and buy soap and salt for my mom. On my way, I saw a convoy of cars coming and the road thick with dust where you couldn't see what was coming, and in the air, there was a fleet of three helicopters circling our village and everyone was scared to death because no one knew what was going on. Amin's soldiers were everywhere blocking off certain routes, so we were in the dark as to what was going on.

Little by little, word got out the helicopter that had been circulating had brought the dead body of Amin's wife, which was being brought back to her parents for burial, and it was rumored that Amin had killed her and sealed her body in the coffin and had ordered that the coffin should never be opened. It was the Amin's soldiers who brought the body back to her parents' home and conducted the burial without anyone seeing the body of the girl. It was the worst experience of my life as a young child. People around that home and the nearby neighbors run away, including my family, for fear that Amin may order his soldiers to start killing people in the community. I remember running with my Dad at night and hiding under the thick bush with just a few tattered clothes on me. It was cold and there were a lot of mosquitoes biting us. We spent all night in the bush and just came back home briefly to look for something to eat and drink before disappearing back to the bush. This continued for several days while the soldiers were left behind to guard the burial ground so that no one can attempt to mess with the grave.

As a young man, I began to think my goals and dreams would not be attained, and I started to doubt whether I should continue to go to school or not. I remember asking my mother that question as to why I should continue to go to school when the dictator Idi Amin was going to kill everyone anyway, but Mom and Dad being very strong parents did what all Mom do best to make sure they assured their children that everything will be okay. I remember Mom telling me, "Son, Amin will not kill everyone. God will not allow that to happen so I should continue to go to school and get my education and gain knowledge. One day, I will be the one to help the people of my community and my beloved country Uganda, Mom said to me with conviction and assurance, looking into my eyes and said, "Son, everything will be okay. Do not worry. God will protect us from this dangerous man, and nothing would happen to us."

Immediately, I believed my mom. I felt a sense of relief and peace and comfort, and I began to think about all my goals. My mother said something that stuck in my mind during my life. Mom said I should never think of letting my dream slip away from me. The only time I should let my dream slip away is only when I die, because that will be the only time, I wouldn't be able to get back up again told pursue my dream, but all other obstacles are temporary. Mom said it would always be a rough road to pursue my dream. I will always encounter difficulties in life but that should never stop me from following my dream. Mom said I would one day fall, but when that happened, I should get up fast, dust myself off, and move on.

Mom's assurance in life gave me the wisdom to maintain a positive outlook in life. I looked at my problems as temporary obstacles that could be overcome and then move on. There is always that small quiet voice in my mind telling me I would be okay and reminding me to remember what Mom and Dad told me when I was young. The voice became part of me because I was constantly being reminded in my mind that I never wanted to let my parents down because I saw how hard they work to raise twelve of us.

Dictator Idi Amin continued to kill the Langi people over the cause of his eight years of rule of Uganda. Innocent people were killed for no apparent reason other than we belonged to the tribe of former president Dr. Milton Obote. I remember one day the rumor was circulating in the villages and the town of Lira the nearby city where I lived that the dictator Idi Amin Dada had ordered all the males of the Langi tribe must be killed. When I was told by my parents of the news as a young child, I was scared and frightened, and I didn't know what to do.

The entire community was terrified by the news and nobody knew what to do. The community hard that Amin has ordered his soldiers to come and killed all the Langi men because they were planning to overthrow his government with the help of the former president Dr. Milton Obote who was already in exile. Dictator Idi Amin Dada was the chief of staff for Dr. Milton Obote who hailed from the city of Lira. Idi Amin Dada overthrew the democratically elected government chosen by the will of the people of Uganda and turned the Uganda government toward military rule. Every rule of law was commanded by military rule, and everyone in Uganda was talking about Sharia Law. As a young child, I didn't understand what the term meant back then and as grew up, I learned it meant a Muslim philosophy of law meaning tit-for-tat law. The dictator Idi Amin Dada was practicing the Muslim faith, and I remember during that time of Amin's rule the people of Langi tribes I was afraid of the people who were practicing Muslim religion because I thought that many were like Dictator Idi Amin Dada and were willing to kill me.

We were told by our parents not to associate ourselves with the Muslim people, regardless of who that person was because we may not know whether that person is a good Muslim or not, every Ugandan who was not a Muslim feared Muslim people at that time. Before Dictator Idi Amin Dada came into power, Ugandan people were living in harmony with each other regardless of their religion and tribe. There were many religions in Uganda, there was freedom of worship in Uganda you could worship anything as your God, and no one minded. Every Christian was getting along very well with Muslim people and other major religions in Uganda with no problem. Everyone in the community practicing their religion, and at one time of the year, all the faiths came together to celebrate their god and faith. There was that practiced of interfaith in the community where all would come together and have the celebration together and eat and drink together with no problem but when Dictator Idi Amin came to power that changed drastically. Amin's changed the view of the Muslim religion in Uganda. At that time, no one in our community wanted to associate themselves with the Muslim religion. We came to view Islam as ungodly religion that was willing to kill people in the name of God. As a young boy, I remember another rumor was circulating that Amin was going door to door looking for Langi men to kill each of them, leaving children and women as orphans and widows, and that scared everyone in the community. I remember my Dad and my brothers began sleeping in the bush at night in fear that Amin's soldiers would come at night and kill us all.

We slept outside in the bush for a month, suffering the coldness at night and mosquito bites. When the sun rose in the morning, we would be shivering due to hypothermia. I was scared that time. I knew that was the end of our life with our family. Dad was a strong man. He made sure to tell us that we would go through this difficult time in our life and would come out victorious and stronger and have a better life. God will not let us die because we have done nothing wrong in his eyes. The strong faith that my parents had helped us to overcome all the t challenges that we had in our lives, and it made us all strong and to believe that there is no problem so big that God would not be able to see us through, and I was glad that our parents were able to have such strong faith in God to lead us through and to be able to guide all their twelve children to the path of freedom and richness in our thinking and that one day God will provide to us ways forward and to have a positive outlook in life that things will one day be all right, no matter how long it took, we would get there one day. Mom and Dad had constantly made us his children to rediscover ourselves in ways we even don't know. Every positive word that came out of their mouth made us better people every day.

It made our eyes and minds see the world in a simple way. And, as I look back now as an adult, Mom and Dad were doing their job as parents by trying to shield their children from the wrong that was going in the world especially in Uganda and Mom and Dad wanted the best of us growing up and above all they wanted us to be kids without worrying so much of what tomorrow will bring to us.

The Amin era was the most challenging time to grow up as a child in Uganda. All essential goods like soap, salt paraffin, sugar, were all not available people were eating food with no salt. No one was drinking tea because there was no sugar to add to the tea. There was no communication system except the radio, which was control by the dictator Idi Amin Dada government, the country, and the people of Uganda were living in darkness. No one knew what was going on in their surroundings, and the only time we learned the news is when someone came and us what they had learned. No one could tell you where the rumors came from, so you took the word as they came to you. The entire country was turned back to the dark ages. Teachers were afraid to stay at school to teach the children for fear that they too can be victims of Dictator Idi Amin's killing machines, the military men who killed without mercy.

There was a rumor that there was a house in Lira that Amin's soldiers designated for killing people and that once you were captured, you were taken there and tortured before you were killed and buried to secret graves at a secret location where no one could find the body. People claimed the house was built underground so that no one could find it. Dictator Idi Amin's rule lasted for eight years, but those eight years felt like an eternity. He said he was going to rule Uganda forever, and no one believed that Amin would leave power. All the Uganda prayed to God for the government of Dictator Idi Amin to come to an end because there was too much killing of innocent people, and all the Ugandans were suffering.

The entire nation was in mourning, and God saw how his children were suffering, and God mobilized his army through the help of the Tanzanian army, and the Kenyan army to came and fight and remove the dictator Idi Amin from power, when the people of northern Uganda hard of the news that there was fighting going on to the Ugandans boarders to try and come and remove the Dictator Idi Amin from power, the news was received with joy and happiness, and I remember as a child seeing my parents and the people of my community celebrating with joy and happiness others were crying of joy and others were fasting for two days, believing that by doing so God would give the power and superiority of weapons that the Tanzanian army and Kenyan soldiers were using to overpower the Dictator Idi Amin's soldiers and then they would come and liberate all of Uganda from this tyrannical ruler.

When Amin's soldiers were attacked, and the fighting broke out and there was a full war going on in Uganda the situation went from bad to worst. Amin'ss soldiers started killing indiscriminately because they knew it was the former president, Dr. Milton Obote, behind the war to try to come and overthrow his government. Dr. Obote hailed from our tribe Langi whom Idi Amin Dada overthrew his government in a coup. Amin knew he was the one now trying to come back and overthrow him, so the Langi tribe was now in danger of being wiped out by Amin's soldiers. Everyone was scared and did not know what to do.

The Tanzanian and the Kenyan soldiers kept fighting to overthrew the Idi Amin Dada Government, to liberate the people of Uganda from dictatorial rule, one by one each town in Uganda was liberated by the Tanzanian army and the Kenyan army, and Amin's soldiers were being killed at an alarming rate on the front lines, and many of his soldiers began to defect from the front lines running for their lives, and some of them took their children with them, fearing that if they are found by the Tanzanian soldiers and Kenyan soldiers they would be killed. So, they began to escape with their families and began the long journey trip back home to their home villages in northern Uganda, as well.

In that process, a lot of them were killed on their way back to their home villages. Women and children suffered due to the war. Many walked for hundreds of miles without food and water to drink, and many died on their way back home since they were too weak to walk such long distances to reach their hometowns. Some were eaten by the wild animals while walking barefoot through the game park where wild animals live, so many were eaten by lions, leopards, and hyenas.

As a young child, it was difficult to see the magnitude of people suffering and dying on the road because they cannot find something to eat and drink. I remember my mother and father gathered the people in our village to discuss what they can do to help the fleeing women and children of the dictator Idi Amin Dada's soldiers who were in dire need of help with food and water on their way home to their villages after the Tanzanian and Kenyan soldiers have now defeated them militarily on many battlefields to liberate the Ugandans from the tyrannical rule.

There was no option for the soldiers apart to begin to start fleeing and save their lives and the lives of their children. Mom and Dad wanted the community to come together and practice their faith, to forgive the Amin's soldiers for what they have done to the Langi tribe by killing them and show them that the Langi people had a good heart. Mom and Dad had a plan to organize the people of our community to collect water in containers and put them on the road for the fleeing soldiers and their families to drink and to place mangoes in the same way so that many can drink and eat the fruit to give them the energy to sustain them during their journey back to their home villages and also to provide the pregnant mothers and young children that were walking all those long distances the energy for them to continue their journey until they reach their final destination, which would be their home village.

I remember as a child Dad and Mom's ideas were met with resistance from the members within the community because many thought it was a bad idea to help the fleeing army of the dictator Idi Amin Dada with food since many will be desperate and would want to kill the Langi people. So, very few people in our community bought into the idea of helping the fleeing soldiers with their children with food and water, but I remember that did not deter Mom and Dad from their plan to practice their faith for forgiveness and doing good to God's children. Mom and Dad could not see the young innocent children pass by them dying of hunger and thirst. They began collecting water and fruits and leave them by the roadside where women and children of Amin's soldiers were passing by for them to find and eat and drink. Mom continued to do this every day while hundreds and hundreds of Amin's soldiers were running for their lives. Every day, they would fill the pot with clean drinking water, and within minutes that water would be gone because many children were thirsty and hungry and there was nothing that could be done so many children began to die on the roadside because they were hungry and weak and thirsty. Pregnant mothers delivered their babies on the roadside and some died with their babies alongside w them and the dead bodies were left on the roadside. As a young child, I was really affected by seeing that many people dying on the roadside and rotting because no one could bury them with the local community, fearing that the Amin's soldiers would come and attack the village.

All the people were in hiding from Amin's soldiers that were fleeing. They didn't want to be seen, but the soldiers themselves were too weak to fight they did not have food to eat many were sick and exhausted from the long walk and many more hundreds of miles to travel before they could reach their final destination. The soldiers did not have cars or trucks to travel in. The army's cars and trucks were old or not serviced, so many of them got mechanical problems and broke down on the roadside, leaving and the soldiers with no options but to abandon the trucks and continue on foot with their children and women. It was a sad time for all the Ugandans to see that much suffering, to the millions of people with no help, Uganda was a dark country because there was no communication and no movement of people because of they feared they would be killed.

At that time human life was valueless. Death became the norm within the communities because death was everywhere you went. Many villagers were dying in large numbers since there were no hospitals that were functioning to help the sick and the dying. The ones that were open the medical equipment were looted by the military and left without medication and drugs to treat diseases, and the nurses and the doctors to care for the sick were nowhere to be seen because of the fear that Amin's soldiers would come and kill them. There were rumors spreading like wildfire that Amin's soldiers were raping and killing all the nurses they found helping and working in the hospital.

During the time the war was going on, there was nowhere that medicine or drugs could be brought into the country, and the fact that Uganda is a landlocked country with no ports of its own made it even harder to get emergency supplies. Uganda relied on Kenyan and Tanzania ports to bring in their goods and services to their people. Since Uganda didn't produce much of their manufactured goods, they had to be imported from the neighboring countries like Tanzania and Kenya, and since the Kenyan and the Tanzanian armies were the one helping the Ugandan army to fight and remove the dictator Idi Amin from power, the government of Tanzania and Kenya decided to close their borders not to allow any good or services to enter Uganda. This made it difficult to find essential goods like salt, soap, clothes, sugar in the market and the inflation on those goods went over 1000 percent because of the scarcity of those essential products.

I remember we were eating food without salt and the food was tasteless and as a child, we were refusing to eat our food because Mom had refused to add salt in our food even if our parents tried to explain to us the reasons why we didn't have salt in our food as children, we refused to accept their explanation. We just simply thought Mom and Dad just didn't want us to have salt in our food, and I remember my younger sister crying so hard on top of her lungs, asking for salt in her food.

There was no soap for bathing or washing. People smelled dirty because they were having to wear the same clothes repeatedly without washing them for months. Some people went to the extent of using herbal plants for bathing which led to several skin diseases and cancer, and some resulted in death reported in some other communities because of using herbal plants. Many developed skin cancer and skin rashes as a result of using toxic plants. Some areas reported blindness as result of using toxic plants to wash their body and faces. I remember me and my younger sister were told by our mother to use pawpaw leaves to wash our clothes. Mom and Dad told us to go and harvest pawpaw leaves and come and boiled them in hot water and that when the water reached the boiling point, we should throw the leaves in the hot water and the foam would come out and that foam we would be able to use for washing our clothes, and the rest we will be able to bathe with, but I remember that was the worst experience in my life. I have never experienced something like that in my life because it turned out that pawpaw leaves are very corrosive and itchy, and when we used the leaves to wash our bodies, my sister and I developed a very painful itchy rash. We scratched all our bodies, and we bled terribly, and the pain was so unbearable we cried all night because of the pain of scratching.

We cried to mom and dad to provide us with medical relief that could stop our body from itching but unfortunately, there was none of that since the country was at war, and it was because of the war that our mom and dad took the drastic step to tell us to use pawpaw leaves to wash our clothes and our body because she did not have other alternatives to help her children. The hospitals were abandoned by the doctors for the fear that Amin's soldiers would come and kill them, since other doctors were already killed by the Amin's soldiers and the nurses too also vacated the hospital, and the patients were left on the floor to wait for their time to die, it was horrific and inhumane treatment of God's children, and the darkest days in Uganda's history, and I hope will not see such kind of treatment of humankind in my lifetime.

CHAPTER 8:
Mom and Dad Lesson of Love to their 12 children

~~~⌒୨~~~

WHILE THIS WAS going on as a young child, I learned at an early age that we all would one day die and that we must work hard and make a positive contribution to this beautiful world we live in. Then, when the time came to die, we would leave the world a better place, and for me as a young child during that time seeing people of my age dying on the street was something I couldn't comprehend, and I began to ask myself why they allowed that to happen to children at such early age, and I asked my mother why did they have to kill innocent young children. She explained to me there are bad people out there who do bad things to innocent people and that we should avoid being with those people and that we should associate ourselves with good people.

Mom and Dad were very smart. They were determined that bad events would not deter us from pursuing our dreams. They always turned a bad situation into a lesson to teach us how life can become complicated, but my mother and father advised us that such life lessons should teach us a very important lesson, which would help us when we become and adults. There would be no problem we would not be able to solve. Mom and Dad turned Dictator Idi Amin Dada's atrocities into a life lesson to teach us to work even harder so that we could be the next generation to bring peace and love to the community where we live. They taught us that we should not show hate towards anybody because we are one people, regardless of what that person looks like or what language that person speaks, or the color of their skin we are all equal before God and that we are all children of God. Mom and Dad had a strong faith in God, and their faith guided them in all that they did and the decisions they make for their family. They were God-fearing a couple, and all their lives were entrusted to God.

Mom and Dad taught us to love and to be loved Mom and Dad taught us to love the people who may hate us for no apparent reason, and, in school, children can sometimes be mean to us because we wore torn uniforms because Mom and Dad could not afford to buy for us new ones, but Mom and Dad taught us to showed love to them and demanded that always we should ask for forgiveness if we did wrong to our friends, and it was an amazing thing to see how our parents who had never gone to school guide us children to do the right thing all the time and always demand from us to d the right thing as Christian children and God's children, and above all my parents wanted us all their children to grow up as God-fearing children because they knew that by living a God-fearing life it will lead us to live a good life which will better the community we leave in.

I remember Dad and Mom telling us that Amin's soldiers were not bad people. They were just following orders. And I remember Dad and Mom saying that those people would pay for their sins against humanity for killing innocent people. I remember Mom and Dad kneeling to pray for Amin's soldiers, that God will open their hearts and minds to let them see the wrong they were doing and the pain and suffering they were causing to the innocent people of Uganda, and they prayed to God to grant them forgiveness because they did not know what they were doing.

During the Amin rule, human life was cheap. Unwarranted killing was rampant. People were killed for no apparent reason. I remember going to the nearby town of Lira with my father and mother and my sisters and brothers, and on the way back home, we saw bodies of dead people lying on the roadsides, rotting with flies covering them. I was in disbelief. As a child, I did not know what to make of it, but that memory stayed in my mind forever and now it still gives me chills. At night when I sleept, I was always having nightmares; the vision of those dead people comes right back at night, and I did not know how to get them out of my mind.

As a child growing up, the images of those dead people made me fear anybody wearing army uniforms, and anybody carrying guns brings back all those memories. So, as children growing up, when we saw army men with guns, we ran as fast as we could to avoid them meeting with us or even seeing us because we knew that if we didn't run away, they would kill us, but that was just simply the fear and emotional trauma we have received as children by witnessing killing at an early age by the Amin's soldiers.

I remember the main road to our town was abandoned. No one was walking on the dusty road, fearing t they'd be caught by Amin's soldiers and get killed. Children feared for their lives. We did not know what to do, apart from what our parents were telling us to avoid getting killed by Amin's soldiers. It was the darkest time of our lives growing up where the sounds of gunfire could be heard from everywhere. Every day, we wondered if that day might be our last on earth because truly, we thought we would be killed by soldiers roaming the streets and patrolling the roads across the country.

There was sexual violence against women found on the street. Often, they were gang-raped by soldiers. Amin's soldiers had ordered that no women could wear mini dresses. If any women were caught wearing the minidress, they were punished by beatings on their buttocks, and many women suffered a lot during that dark time in Uganda. Many women were afraid of Amin Dada's soldiers, and many women and men alike feared for their life and their safety. They were not free to enjoy their lives. Women felt their lives controlled by the government of Idi Amin Dada. There was no freedom of speech or freedom of choice. Every citizen felt controlled by the government. You cannot criticize the government of Amin, and all who try to do it paid with their life. Many Ugandan people felt enslaved in their own country.

Children in Uganda at that time gave up hope in life and many felt there was no need to go to school or further their education because the hope and dreams were not there. Every child knew they were either going to get killed or their parents were going to be killed by Amin Dada's soldiers, so many felt there was no need for education. One day when we went to school early in the morning and found teachers packing their bags and some few belongings in backpacks, and teachers with young children putting their young ones on their backs, and men putting children on their shoulders, ready to take a long journey deep into the jungle to where their parents lived, and they'd be safe from Amin's soldiers.

Many people had little or nothing at all to eat or drink for their children. I remember seeing young children crying for food, but their parents couldn't provide for them. The very young children were breastfed, but their mother's breast milk was not enough. Many mothers had not eaten food for two days and breast milk can't be produced. It was a scary thing to witness, seeing a mother helpless to their children and seeing the pains in the mother's face because she could not help her crying children. As a young child myself, I couldn't even describe the pain and fear in my mind. I was so terrified. I didn't know what was going to happen to me and my parents. The fear that my parents would be killed, and we as siblings will be left alone to fend for ourselves was so overwhelming for a young child because we saw our mother and father as providing us with all what we need as children to grow up, and the provider for all our needs. We couldn't imagine losing our parents at such a young age. Our father and mother were the sole winners of bread, food, water, clothes, salt, and soap. they labored day and night to struggle to provide these essential goods to their twelve children, and we couldn't imagine without my mother and father what we could have done to get these essential goods to all twelve siblings.

I remember one time we had to eat food without salt for months and months because the salt price had gone up and our mother and father could not afford it. As children, we turned to our mom to ask why this was happening, and Mom had to explain what was going on, but as children, we couldn't accept what the explanation was from our father. What we wanted was to get salt in our food, and I remember my younger sister refused to eat food provided to her by our mother unless salt is added to her food. At that time, I saw the pain in our mother's eye because she was helpless and had done her best to explain to her children the reasons as to why we had no salt in our food. As young children, however, no matter much she explained the problem to us, we were not ready to accept her explanation, and our refusal to accept our mother's explanation caused pain to our mother and father. Looking back as an adult and seeing it from my children.

I can now understand it as being a typical behavior for young children, and as an adult with children of my own, I am left wondering the pain I saw on my mother and father's faces as a result of us refusing to accept our parents' explanation or because our parents felt they had let their children down since they could not provide all that is needed for their children or maybe our parents thought they were not good parents simply because they could not provide mere salt in the food for their children, but as I grew up and had children of my own now, I understood why my father and mother felt that way we all want to see our children happy, and it's always difficult to explain to our kids as to why we are in a situation we are in. Neither Father nor Mother had no formal education, but both had common sense and decency to instill good values in their children. Their common sense guided them very well, they knew the importance to sit us all down every evening around the fireplace in our yard and explain to their twelve children the important values in life, and one of the values our parents instilled in us during those fireplace gatherings was the importance of family and what family meant to them.

Our family made us aware that there is nothing important in life than being together and loving each other unconditionally, without materialistic things. Just showing love to one another and enjoying the company of one another was more than having the material wealth that the world can offer. Mom and Dad made us feel so valuable and loved despite the abject poverty we were living in. They made us feel human in our lives. They made us forget our hunger, starvation, and scary feelings of not having what we need as children. They made us feel the sense of belonging at a time when felt we were nobody. My parents made us discover our self-worth what we want to do with our life when we grew up, and they made us think beyond what we wanted to achieve in life despite the fact there was no means to get to what we want to achieve in life or the supporting material that would help us achieve the goals we have in mind. I did credit our mother and father for not saying anything negative about our dreams.

All twelve of us children had a different dream in life of what we wanted to accomplish in our lifetimes, and when we all gathered in the evening around the fire in front of our mud grass thatch mud hut prepared by our mother and father. As children, we started to talk about different aspirations or different things we would like to do when we grew up, while our father and mother listened to us all, and I wonder what they were thinking at that moment when they were listening to us, about their big dreams but knowing that they were not able to provide or support any of their twelve children's dreams since they were living in abject poverty in a small grass thatch hut built with mud with no running water, no electricity, and that must have really caused pain and suffering in my mom and dad's hearts. It's hurtful to be poor, and it's hurtful to have good, intelligent children that unable to support them through their goals and dreams, and I always wondered if my father and mother's health was affected by these worries.

They wanted to see the best come to their twelve children, but they were unable to provide financial support since they were so poor. Despite their abject poverty, our father and mother never discouraged us from pursuing our dreams. They wanted to see the best in us. Mom and Dad were the sources of strength and courage for all their twelve children, both my mom and my dad treated all of us equally. They both showed us unconditional love. I remember as a child waking up very early in the morning running up to my mother telling her I was very hungry, and I needed something to eat. At that moment, Mom didn't have any food or anything to give me to calm me down, and I started to cry for food, and at that moment, I saw my mother's face turn green and her face was not joyful, and I knew there was something wrong.

My mother seemed powerless because she could not provide food to her crying baby. As I recall now what pain my mother was going through in her heart, I remember my continuing to cry all that morning nonstop and waking up other brothers and sisters of mine who were sleeping, and all the other kids join in the crying because they too were hungry, and they wanted food to eat. At that very moment, I thought to myself why our mother cannot give us food or anything to drink because as a child nothing else could stop you if you need something you need it to be provided to you. So, all of us kids early in the morning needed something to eat and drink but our mother at that moment couldn't provide food or something to drink. The fastest thing our mother could do was to go to the kraal and milk the cow and give to us warm milk to drink since that would be the fastest way to calm us all down, but Mom couldn't do that because it was still very dark in the morning. So she waited for daybreak to go to the kraal to milk the cows and bring to us some warm milk to drink and fill our bellies.

I remember I was so happy seeing my mother coming back home with some milk in the jar and pouring it in the plastic cup to me and my brothers and my sisters to drink. It was the happiest moment for us, and we knew Mom had again provided the needed milk to us to keep us all nourished for that day, and, at that moment, I remember Mom pouring some milk in another container and telling us that if we got hungry again while she is still tending the garden with my father, we could go ahead and pour the milk in a cup and drink it, but she also made sure we were not selfish, so Mom told us that if there wasn't enough milk for all of us, we should make sure we shared what little milk there among ourselves so that everyone got something to keep our stomachs quiet until they get back from the garden and come and could prepare for us something to eat for that day.

Our mother was everything to us, she was the best mother one could ever ask for. She knew how to calm us all in times of crisis. She knew her children's individual needs and that all our needs were different, and because of that understanding, she was able to attend to us all with respect and dignity, and we were able to give her all the respect and love she deserved as our mother. She was able to manage the twelve of us with ease. She was a kind and loving mother, who respected the dignity of all humankind. She was firm and decisive in her decision-making, as well as clear and precise in her communication to her children. Our father was the disciplinarian who made sure all of us behaved in a manner that always gave respect to our mother and the adults around us. As a result of that, our family was given respect in the community. We won the hearts of many people in the village with good behavior, even though we were poor.

We didn't complain to anyone or going around begging anything from our fellow villagers, although the children within our community were raised as a team in which any child in our community could go to anybody's house and eat food or drink some water without fear. We all grew up with that sense of we are one people in one community.

As a young child growing up with my beloved parents, I always wonder why God created me to be born to a poor family, and I continued to wonder whether people had a choice to be born in a rich or poor family, but as I grew up and began to understand things around me, I realized that was not the case. I became angry about what I was going through while being powerless to do anything to change my situation. Also, I did not want to blame my parents for what I was going through because I knew my parents were the best parents anyone could have asked for, and I knew at a young age that our parents loved us unconditionally, and if they had the means to support us, they would provide for us, but unfortunately, they did not have the means to do so.

I continued to learn that human beings had no choice as to which family they would be born to. That life is a gift from God to any parent. Then, I began to ask myself several questions, like, "Why do some families have material things and other families don't?" It was unfair that all the poor children like me had to go through what we went going through without much help from the people in leadership because children deserve to have a happy childhood, and they deserve to have food, clothes, shelter, warmth, shoes on their feet, a blanket to keep them warm at night, and a good house to protect them at night from wild animals and dangerous predators that roam around at night. Above all, these children deserve to have as good an education as children from well-to-do families.

I remember when I was nine years old, our father woke us up before in the morning to go and help him in the garden plant cabbages and tomatoes, which he grew for food and for sale to earn money to support us all and buy us clothes and pay for our education. I remember me and my four sisters woke up and went with our Dad to the garden to help with planting tomato seed in the nursery bed and transferring the cabbage seedlings from the nursery beds to plant them in the garden. I remember it was a long day at work that day. My four sisters and I were so hungry and thirsty, but we didn't have anything to eat and drink at that moment. We were all weak and drained, and I remember my sister wanted to fall due to thirst and hunger, but we were powerless again. We didn't have the means to do anything to help us in the situation we were in because at the same time we did not want to feel that we have let our father and mother down because they were so close to our heart. We all knew that Dad and Mom wanted the best of us, and they were doing what they could to help us grow up to be good citizens and productive children within our community.

My four sisters and I stayed until midday in the garden helping our parents. It was very hot sunshine of the tropics, so it was exhausting and tiresome to walk home since we have little energy left on our body to make the trip. I remember the only thing that was in all in our minds was to get cold drinking water but that was even difficult to get because Mom and Dad had to walk a distance to go and fetch the water and remember thinking to myself this is such a difficult life to go through as a young little boy. I wanted not to go through the life my parents were going through. I wanted a better life for myself and my family when I grew up, and those life experiences help to shape my thinking on how I wanted my life to be. I remember one day I was coming back from helping my parents from the garden work and I was tired and exhausted too so I sat down under a mango tree, thinking what I should do with my life to make things better for me and my family. I remember a quiet voice that came to my mind and said, "It is only you who can change the destiny of your own life, and it is only you who can do what is good for yourself not anyone else will come and do it for you. So, the question I am putting to you now is what do you want to do with your life and what do you want your life to be in five years, ten years from now, twenty years from now, and thirty years from now? Please figure out the answers to these questions for yourself."

When I was fully rested under the mango tree and gained some strength, which would take me back home. I started asking myself the answers to these questions. I remember this was a serious matter, and I needed to think about it and figure out what I wanted to do for myself and what I would want my life to be in five years, ten years, fifteen years, twenty years, twenty-five years, thirty years, but I didn't know what came to my mind at that time would be called the "goals." I was too young to figure out my logical thinking, at seven years old when the love for your parents is undeniable. It's so strong you see your parents as everything to you and you do not want anything to happen to them so seeing my parents going through this hard labor to support us break my heart to the point that sometimes I go and hide myself in the nearby bush and started to cry uncontrollably because I wanted the suffering to stop and have a better life and enjoy life and be happy like other kids are doing. In my mind as a child, I thought crying my eyes out would change things or will make things better, so I continued to cry, hoping my cry would change things, but it was all in vain, so I decided now to continue to think how I would make my life better and how I should go about it.

It was a tough decision for a young child to take, but without a doubt, I knew that if I put my mind into something and work hard for it, I would be able to achieve the goal I wanted to achieve, so I started thinking towards what I had thought under the mango tree, exhausted from having work so hard with my parents in the garden plowing the filed. I started thinking that I was already seven years old and attended second grade, so I decided that if I needed a better life for myself and my family there was no other way out except that education was the only key and the way out to address our family problems.

My parents wanted us all to have an education, but they were too poor to pay for the cost of schooling for all twelve children. Although they were illiterate themselves, they knew the benefit of education. As a child of seven, I was already mature in my thinking because of what I have gone through. I didn't have time to be a child playing around like other children would do at seven years old. When I was at home, I was either helping my parents tend to the garden or looking after the cows or pronging cotton, so I didn't have time to play with other children. When I turned eight years old, that is when my mind open up and started to follow what was in my mind and that was when I started to think seriously about what I want to do and what I wanted to see my life to be in the future, and I started to think big in terms of what I wanted to see in our family. Most importantly, I wanted to see smiles on my mother and my father's faces once in a while, and I did not know what I was going to do to bring that smile to their faces because their faces were full of sorrow, despair, agony, and fear at all times because they struggled every day to work hard to support us twelve children.

The stressful situation my mother and father were in was unbearable to anybody, but I wonder how my mother and father were able to overcome such a difficult situation and raised all of us twelve children to grow to adulthood, because everywhere we turned, we surrounded by poor families, friends, relatives, aunts, uncles, grandmothers, and grandfather were all poverty-stricken and were all barely making ends meet. At eight years old, when I sat under that mango tree thinking what I should do to better my life and my family life, especially for my mother and father who worked so hard every day to take care of us. So, I decided to come up with a plan, and the plan was for me to stick with education, and I knew at an early age that if I needed to come out of the poverty and lead a better life my only hope was going to be to hold on to education so tight and not let go, like when you climb high up to the top of a tree. You hold on to the branches of the tree so tightly because any slight mistake you make will cost your life, so I decided I will glue myself onto education and never let go, and I wanted to make myself proud within our community, and, above all, I wanted my parents to be proud of me and help them, but I didn't know how I was going to accomplish that because I had to help my parents in the garden every morning and to look after cows and goats every day morning and night, but I was determined to make it work for me.

When I had turned nine, I told my mother and father that I wanted to concentrate on my education and have a better life for our family and to be able to help them as well. I remember when my mother heard me saying those words of wanting to have a good education to help them, she was overwhelmed and cried tears of joy. When I was thinking of communicating this message to my parents, I didn't how they were going to react, because both of my parents were illiterate. They didn't have formal education, but they were smart and well-equipped with common sense to help guide all their twelve children.

My mother told me, "My son, I will support you all the way whatever you decide to do. I will be there for you all the time you need my help." I remember hearing those words of comfort and support coming from my beloved mother. I was overcome with joy and tears of joy rolled down my cheeks, and we cried together with my mother. I was expecting a negative reaction from my mother like, "When you go to school, then who will help look after the livestock?" or I was expecting my mother to say education was a waste of time because they didn't have the means to pay or I was expecting my mother to say reply that I should stay home and help my father prepare the garden for the next harvest or I was expecting my mother to say education was a waste of time. I should just stay home and wait to get married to a sweetheart girl that will come and help the family in the garden and make local drink liquor called "waragi" brewed and consumed in my community, but instead, my mother gave me unconditional support and love in my quest to get an education, even though they didn't have the means to pay, and that unconditional love from my mother encouraged me and made me feel good.

It is a testament to all the poor children out there in a similar situation like mine need that unconditional love and support from their parents so that they can follow up on their dreams, and they need to hear from their parents the word of love, support, and encouragement that they can do anything they put their mind to, regardless of their parents' ability to pay for the cost of their education. My mother and my father were my role models. They never complained to anybody about their situation. Instead, they were role models to the women and men in our community because my mother and my father worked together to solve their problem in their house, and it was amazing growing up to see my mother and father working together to come up with a solution to a problem deemed difficult for a person living without any daily income at all except their food stored in the local granary or the food that is still in the garden not yet harvested, but they tackled any problems that came their way together as husband and wife> they consulted each other on any situation facing their family and worked out a way to address that situation affecting their family and resolve the problem together as one person tight in the bond of marriage. It was so comforting to see my mother and father working together and seeing the love between the two. As young children growing up, we were full of joy and comfort to see the love that existed between our father and mother.

CHAPTER 9:
Chasing the Dream of a Better Life

~~

I WOULD DESCRIBE MY father's reaction to my quest for education as peaceful, without comment. He didn't say anything to me, but I knew he wanted the best of me as well, and also I knew that since my mother had full support for my education, my father was also down to fully support my school ambitions, but what gave my Dad pause in supporting my ambitious quest for my education was how he was going to afford to pay for it, because I figured he can barely support all the twelve children financially, and because the only resources he had were to feed the children, never mind the cost of education, which was very expensive as the government in Uganda, which did not have the public school for children from poor families.

I knew it was going to be difficult for my father to support my education, but I knew that if I and my father and my mother work very hard, we were could and achieve the goal of my education. When I was in the fourth grade, I laid down my goals to achieve my level of education. My first goal was to make sure I worked hard and overcame the challenges that might stop me from graduating from primary seventh and going on to secondary school because that level of education was when the primary school children of my community dropped out of school or were removed by their parents to help their parents if they are boys, or if they are girls, they are removed by their parents to stay home and wait to get married at the young age of twelve years so that the parents could get bride price to help the families with their poor living conditions.

Most of my young friends dropped out of school at twelve years old to get married, and many told me I was wasting my time and my parents' money because I was going to go nowhere with my education, and I was going to break my parents' hearts with all the hard work they are putting in to send me to school, selling all their food to pay for my education, the food they would have fed with our brothers and sisters, but I was determined in my quest to get an education and have a better life to support my family and have a better life for myself. So, nothing that any of my friends or people within my community say was going to deter or stop me from my quest to get my education. It was a difficult task that I had set for myself because of the living condition we were living in with no electricity or running water. I had no lights at night to help me with my reading at night.

When nighttime came, we were left completely in the dark. The only light came from burning firewood to provide us with heat at night and light. I remember dad went out to a local market one day and bought a locally made lamp that used kerosene and generated lots of smoke, which caused eye irritation and a burning sensation when the smoke entered your eyes and when it entered your mouth, you coughed badly, but my dad wanted to give me some light to help reading my books at night. The lamp smoke became unbearable. I developed a bad cough and eye problems, which meant I could not see for three weeks and that my mother and father had to take me to the hospital to seek medical treatment for my cough and my eye problem.

I remember the eye doctor telling my father and my mother to tell me to stop using the lamp because it was killing my eyes and causing my cough and the chemicals from the lamp were affecting my eyes and causing me to cough uncontrollably. I was sad to hear this from the doctor. I thought that I was going to lose my eyesight, but I was lucky that I was able to get the treatment early before my eye got completely damaged, but I remember asking my father the question whether the lamp had destroyed my eye completely or I was still going to be able to see after that, the question to my father was to assure me that I was still going to be okay, even though I had the eye problem.

I wanted to hear from my father that I was going to be okay and that nothing will stop me from pursuing my dream goal of getting an education, and the best person to give me that assurance was my father because I trust and love both my mother and father and to be able to get that assurance from my father that everything was going to be okay meant a lot to a growing young man. To hear the words of encouragement, uplifting words, assurance words and to know that your parents both believe you will be okay, and you will be able to make it becomes self-assurance that I would attain my goal. My father was a soft-spoken person. He never yelled at anyone but rather spoke with a calm and determined voice, and when he spoke, we all paid attention and listened to what our father was saying to us and because of that, I came to appreciate him more and more, because he wanted the best of me.

He wanted me to succeed in my quest for my education. He wanted me to be happy and feel proud of myself and not think about our poverty because what matters was that he loved us all unconditionally, so he supported me in every way he could. I never blamed my father in any way as to why he could not provide for my school fees for my education. H had already made me aware that he could not pay for my education because he was so poor, and he had already communicated to me that for us to continue to get the money to pay for my education, we should be able to work together, father and son, by helping him in the garden digging and plowing with the bulls and oxen for people, and people, in return, would pay us some little money for food and some he will save for the school fees for my education or harvesting crops that he had planted in the garden and sell some of the crops to earn money to pay for my education and the education for my brothers and my sisters.

My father made me be aware that he and I would be working together to earn income to support my education. He was there any time I needed help. One day, I started digging my garden near our house to prepare it to plant the cotton for the season to help me pay for my education for the next academic season. The next day, I woke up very early in the morning to go to my garden and till it alone before the sunrise and go to school, but as I started digging my garden I looked up and saw both my parents coming in with their hoes to help me.

My reaction was speechlessness, but in my mind, I was dying to say to my parents, "Thank you for being here to help me," but I was scared to do that to their faces, but I was filled with emotion to know that my parents cared for me so much and love me so much no matter what and to know that they are there for me any time I needed them and that they were supporting me in my goal to obtain my education by waking up in the very early morning to come and help me dig a bigger garden to plant cotton was a testament to me that my parents were there for me all the way to see me succeed.

I was filled with emotion. I wanted to cry to show my appreciation to my parents. That night, when I went to bed, I cried until I couldn't shed any more tears. I was filled with a mixture of sadness and happiness, the sadness of seeing my parents labor so hard to support me and thinking if they were rich, they would not have to work so hard. That broke my heart, and the happiness and joy that filled my heart came from knowing that God created me in a loving family for a reason.

The more I thought about it the more appreciated my family and didn't care whether I was sleeping hungry without food at night or walking naked with no clothes on. I would not blame my parents for that because I knew God had a plan for me, and that plan was more than material things. When my parents came to the garden to help me till my land to plant the cotton for my school fees, I held my tears, and instead, I kept it cool by not crying out loud. Instead, the tears just kept rolling down my cheeks as a grown-up person crying but that didn't stop me from letting both of my parents know how much I loved them, and I appreciated them for what they did for me and what they have done for me and my other brothers and sisters.

I was blown away by the love, kindness, and support my father and mother had shown toward me. They let me know they had no financial support to give me for my education, but they let me know they would be there every step of the way to support me in any way they could. My father and mother continued to help me for several days, tilling the land and preparing it for planting cotton. It was hard labor and very intensive, but my mother and father never ever complained or said anything negative that might've discouraged me. Instead, both were so very happy to help me open this big open land to grow cotton and harvest it to help finance my education.

I woke up very early in the morning every day to weed my cotton in the field before I headed to school. In the evenings, I came back from school and headed up to the cotton field to prune and weed the cotton. I was so determined to achieve my goal, and I knew that when cotton was ready, I would pick it, sort it, and sell it to the cotton cooperative society near our home, and then I would earn some money to pay for my education, but my hopes and dreams came to test when a hailstorm came and destroyed all my cotton. I remember I cried for two weeks every day because I did not know where to turn to or what to do next because that was my only hope of getting money for my education that year.

My mother and father tried their best to console me that things would be okay. I should stop crying, but as a child, I knew there were no other alternatives for me getting money for my education that year because my father and my mother has no means of getting money from somewhere else apart from selling the food they had grown to feed twelve of us, and I did not want to take away food grown to feed my brothers and sisters, so I knew that next year I would not be able to go to school because I will have no means to pay for the school fees for that year.

After crying for many weeks, mourning the loss of my cotton crop I came to realize that there was nothing I could do to get the destroyed plants back, and I had to move on and come up with other ways and means to find money to cover the cost of my education for the next academic year. My father and my mother came and sat me down one day and said, "Son, look the cotton crops are all gone now due to heavy rain. Now, we need to come up with another alternative plan."

The alternative plan from Dad and my mother was to prepare the field to plant sweet potatoes that would grow fast and harvest fast to sell to earn some money for my school fees for next year, so I bought into the idea and we started preparing a new field to plant sweet potatoes, and the plan worked. We grew lots of sweet potatoes in the field, which was enough for our home consumption and some for sale to earn money for my school fees for the year. I was so happy and excited that I was able to fulfill my dream for that year and got the education I so needed badly.

My father and mother were the bedrock to make a miracle happen for my education. They did all they could to make sure I went to school every year, even if they did not know where the money was going to come from to pay for my education, but they knew for sure that they would do what it takes to make sure they get the money to pay for my school fees for the year. When night came, and I was tired and exhausted, I always wondered what I would have done without my beloved mother and father who were the most wonderful parents one would have asked for. Very poor but kind and rich in spirit, the parents that will never pass anybody in our village without greeting and talking to them and asking how they were doing. My parents were full of gratitude and hopes and dreams for their children.

My parents shared and fed many people in our village with the little food they grew to feed their children, but they were always sharing with the people who don't have much, and with that kind spirit, they were blessed with more and more by God. I learned from my father and mother what makes a person great is not wealth or the material things but the heart of giving and sharing what they had with people who have nothing, and I was lucky to be born to a parent who had that heart for caring for one another, and I was lucky enough to learn from my parents to give respect to all the people we come in contact with, be they young, elderly, poor, or rich. People from different religious backgrounds, people who didn't look like me—disabled people, and people who don't speak my language all deserve respect and good treatment because all are created in God's image and all deserved to be loved and respected. I thank my parents for instilling that lesson in me at such a young age and thank them for making me come closer to

God, and I became a responsible adult and instilled that same love of God in my children.

Growing up in total poverty did not change who we were. As children of God, my parents taught us all that regardless of our economic status we are still the lovely children to our creator God, and nothing will stop us from giving praise to him and asking him for guidance. Our parents instilled in us all the importance of being God-fearing in all that we do and that made all of us strong, and we all believed we will all be okay, regardless of growing up in poverty with that strong faith and conviction of a God-fearing family we developed a strong bond loving each one of us, and we saw the humanity in each of us and in all people around us. All the struggles that came our way, we handled together as a family. Any challenges that came our way, we overcame them as a family. Our parents became an inspiration to all their twelve children.

Both our parents became role models to us all the twelve children we look at them of what they were going through to raise twelve siblings without no income at all, but they never complained or mistreated any of us. Our parents let us know that we the twelve siblings are their source of pride and happiness and that became even more important to us all because we knew Mom and Dad loved us all, and we should love them back and that became a very big tool that our parents used to guide and lead us and because of that, we were able to do what our parents wanted us to do.

It became clear to all of our twelve siblings that we were all born in poverty and we would grow up poor, and we had to accept that facts and each of us will have to think and find ways on how we will come out that poverty and lead a productive life as other children are and that was not easy for each of us, because we did not know what to do as children or were to start from but what we knew for a fact is that we needed to all survive but with our parents' guidance and help we as children we began working as a team both to help our parents in all what they do.

Teamwork became so important to twelve children, there was nothing that we were not doing together our parents made sure we were all there together in all aspect of our life and that became the first line of defense on overcoming poverty because we were able to produce food, which was enough to feed twelve of us in the family. All twelve children went and plowed and prepared a big field ready for the planting of crops and my parents were able to harvest enough food for our own consumption enough to feed the family, and the rest for sale to earn some income for our parents to buy some clothes for themselves and some clothes for twelve of us siblings and some money they use for buying soap and some money to buy salt.

Most of the time, there was not enough money, so we had to go without soap for bathing and eat food without salt added, and I remember one day my sisters refused to eat food without salt, and my parents tried to explain to my sisters the reason we had no salt in the food. Being young children, they could not understand my parents' explanation. Tall they understood was that they wanted salt in their food and my parent had none at that moment. To see the pain in the eyes of my parents because they couldn't provide a simple thing as salt to their children's food simply was heartbreaking to see our parents go through that pain just because of something simple as buying salt. That simple experience was important for me as a child. I could not stop thinking about it, and I wanted to do something to change the situation when I grew up. I didn't want my children to go through what I had gone through. I wanted them to have a better life for themselves and not to see the pain in my eyes because I could not afford to buy salt.

The experience was so profound in my life growing up because it was the simple thing that we went through because we were poor and my parents could not afford to buy something simple as salt, so I came to realize that I need to do something about it and I remember I made my mother a promise that when I grew up I would never see her go without salt and water again, and that even made my push for education became even stronger because I wanted to fulfill my promise to my mother.

I was very lucky to be born to parents who are kind-hearted despite their total abject poverty. They had heart of gold they were loved by their community and the people in their area. They taught their children to love strangers and all the people they met. They saw humanity in everyone. They opened their doors to all who are in need our house became the stopover for all who are in need, be it for food, water, or asking for assistance with salt and soap to share to go feed their children.

My parents became angels in our community. They had nothing but they were rich in the spirit of sharing anything in their possession, and as a child this affected me in a big way. We, all twelve children, became symbols of good behavior in our community and all the people in our community loved us, and we love them back, our poverty became ways of our life and became part of us, and we all had to come to terms with it and accept it and move on with our lives. I was so lucky to be born to parents who taught us all the importance of forgiveness at an early age.

We were taught to forgive one another at a tender age. When we disagreed or fought with our siblings, our parents would make sure we ask for forgives from each of us failure to ask for forgiveness from your brother or your sister would lead to further disciplinary steps by our father. These lessons made us better kids growing up and better adults, and the lessons stayed with me forever. As an adult now, I remember what Dad and Mom told us what we need to do when we did something wrong. Always ask for forgiveness, and that will open your heart and make you a better person we are all human and we are liable to make mistakes. So, it became so important to have that heart to ask for forgiveness, and I was glad that my mother and my father despite the abject poverty lived in were able to instill in all of us the great lesson of forgiveness, which has continued to impact our life into our adulthood, and I always wonder if without all the qualities that our mother and father taught us. I wonder whether I was going to succeed to where I am today.

Forgiveness makes you proud of who you are it makes you human and shows you that the other person is human as well and because of that you all become human and know that treat the other person with respect and dignity. My parents taught us the importance of being obedient because through obedience to our parents, we were able to learn from them as much as we could to help us become better siblings, and all the lessons we learned from our parents help us to be better children both in the eyes of the public and the people around us—our neighbor coworkers, friends, and all the people we come in contact with and above all in the eyes of the creator God.

I was lucky to be born to parents with courage and determination and hard work. My mother had the courage to tackle poverty head-on. She didn't let poverty win regardless. She and my father were able to stand up to poverty and fight it head on they both didn't want poverty to win because they had children to feed and people who depend on them every day with no formal education of their own both my parents had the common sense to know what to do to fight poverty they decided the only hope for fighting poverty was to go into farming and grow food for their children and have faith in Jesus Christ and God their creator. My mom and dad had the courage and determination in all that they do, and that courage and determination gave them all the hopes and dreams to dream big and plan big for their twelve children.

Dad and Mom always set two goals for the year. One goal is to plant beans on a large scale and millet on a large scale for home consumption and for sale to help raise money to buy for us essential items or household items, and the second goal was to plant sweet potatoes and cabbages in big quantities for both for sale and consumption. The vegetables like cabbages and sweet potatoes were to subsidize the family income in case the dry weather destroy beans and millet the family would still have something to eat because these crops do not take a long time to grow. Dad and Mom grew a lot of vegetables for sale and to balance our diet since we did not have money to buy other food items to allow us to have the nutrition we need to grow up healthy children.

With little knowledge and no educational background, Mom and Dad made sure they changed our diet every day, so we didn't always eat the same thing. Every day our diet was mostly comprised of vegetables and lots of fruits and greens picked fresh from the farm or wild plants that Dad and Mom knew about, and I always wonder how Mom and Dad knew about these plants they pick from the wild forest and bring home and prepare for us to eat. These experiences taught me and my sisters lots of lessons in life for survival for the fittest. We knew we could survive anywhere in the world if we have our eyes and hands to help us see and work hard.

As children, we all learned how to work hard at a very young age because we were the sole source of manpower for our parents. We all provide labor for our parents on the farm and preparing land ready for planting crops to grow. When harvest time came, all twelve kids were there to help our parents harvest the crops from the garden and carry them home on our heads for storage in the granary to feed us all until the next season of planting crops began, and the same process began once again and again, and I knew this would not stop until any one of our twelve children did something to help our parents and get out of the poverty. I knew that was not going to be an easy thing to do, and I knew it was going to take a lot of sacrifices to get to where I wanted to go, but with all the determination and trust in God that mother and father instilled in all of us, I knew nothing was going to stop me because God would guide me through in all what I would want to do to get out of poverty.

I remember one day I had taken cows and goats and sheep to graze out in the wild. I was so tired that day I had not eaten much the previous day, and I was so hungry and thirsty in the bush, looking after the cows and goats and sheep and besides I had to walk long distances to take the cows to look for grass and water to drink and eat. I remember that day I knelt down under a tree and pray to God specifically to guide me through anything that I wanted to do so that I could take away the pain and suffering I am going through mentally and physically, but also I knew that will not be an easy fix and I knew it will take a long time to reach to where I was asking God to help me on my struggle and the quest for a better life for my family. However, I knew that putting God first in my struggle would calm me in facing whatever obstacle I may come across during my struggle, and to overcome those struggles through the power above me, and I think that work so perfectly because putting God first made me look at things in this world as materialistic things, which you can acquire and can disappear at any time so they became less important to me and that allowed me to concentrate on my goals of obtaining an education.

By putting God first in my life, I was able to see things from a different perspective especially when I was going to school with torn uniforms and bare feet while my fellow children have good-looking uniforms, and shoes on their feet, I was able to overcome the fear and the shame that I was having for myself because my uniform was torn, and I was walking in bare feet. Mom and Dad had always made me aware that in the presence of God. All are equal and the same even if you are walking naked because you could not afford to buy clothes, God still loves you, and you are still the child of God and that biblical teaching really helped me become strong, and I was not afraid to go out there and go to school with my torn uniform and play with my fellow children with no fear or shame with my torn uniform.

When I was praying under the tree looking after the cows and goats and sheep in the wilderness a plane flew over my head and that loud sound scared me to death, but at the same time, it got me thinking about the question that how I can one day be able to be inside the plane, and I started to search for an answer to that question and the answer to my question became obvious that if I wanted to see inside the airplane education would be the only way out for me because both my mom and dad are so poor so that will be out of the equation for them to afford because if they couldn't afford to buy salt or soap or clothes for themselves, there was no way they will be able to afford anything like that so because of all these events that were happening in my life just reaffirmed to me that education was the only key for me for a better life for me and my family, but how to get there was the thing to worry about then.

It became clear to me that education is a fundamental human right that every human being has the right to have inclusive and quality education regardless of their ability to pay for the cost of education to make the most of his or her potential, I started to think why did they make education such an expensive thing which limits the children from the poor family to attend school so I became very inquisitive as to why that was the case, and I came to realize at an earlier age that the benefit of education is far greater and that I should hold on to it I knew that there must be something good that comes out of education for them to make it so expensive for the poor people not to be able to afford.

I continued to struggle with that, thinking as to how education would make my life better and the life of my family. I did not want to use all the resources that my father and mother worked so hard to get and then nothing good come out of it, and I did not want to disappoint my parents, so I kept thinking about how I would continue with this important choice I have made in my life to get an education, but it became clear to me that that was the only hope to get a better life in this world.

With my quest for education, I had lots of challenges all the way long. Sometimes, I had no way to buy books and uniforms that the school need, and sometimes I had no school fees since my parents could not pay the cost of the education, so I was sent back home and stay for two months while my mother and father struggled to get the money for school fees, so when my father managed to get the school fees, they would sometime be late, and I would be behind with my lessons in the syllabus for that year, so I had to do a lot of catching up with my fellow students, but that didn't stop me or discourage me for my quest for education to get a better life.

I had to work extra hard to make sure I catch up with other students who had been all along at school. As I continued with my education, I came to learn that education is one of the decisive levers with which enables people to escape poverty or poverty trap spanning generation, and it became clear to me it is only through education that people gain options, become innovators and are able to take their lives in their hands, and I came to know that education increases the chances of obtaining a permanent job and regular income and that education leads to better living standards and allows people to be able to make long-term plans as well as accepting personal responsibility for themselves.

Also, I became aware that education is an effective and sustainable tool for promoting public health. If you are educated you are better informed about diseases, hygiene, and nutrition. Education helps people recognize the symptoms of diseases earlier and seek medical treatment, and I became better informed. My eyes opened up, and I became aware and I started to wonder if my mother and father had an education they would have really taken care of us better but at the same time I became more thankful and very appreciative of what they have accomplished for us even without the formal education of their own, and finally, I learned that education promoted tolerance mutual understanding and long-term strategic thinking, which allowed one to think what direction they want to lead their life and how to get there and how to achieve that goal.

CHAPTER 10:
My Ticket out of Poverty

EDUCATION BECAME EVERYTHING to me. I knew the only way out of poverty would be through education. I then sacrificed all that my parents had to get an education. I would go hungry in school, but that didn't bother me so much because I knew one day all that would be history. I knew education would one day lead me to the land of the plenty and I would have what I did not have growing up, but I wouldn't be telling the truth if I said that not having all that I needed at school didn't hurt my body.

I know I was weak and thin during my school years because of too much thinking and lack of enough nutritious food to eat because I could not afford to buy those things and because neither my parents nor I had enough money to buy me everything required for school, but I was committed to my education, and nothing was going to stop me from obtaining those goals of obtaining an education. I treated my education as a call from God to acquire the means to relieve my parents and my family from the decade of poverty spanning generations and generations from my family, and I was determined to overcome that barrier and bring joy and happiness to my mother and father and the rest of my family.

It was determined to have a better life for myself and to see my mother and father happy and proud of me. Because of that determination, I was motivated to work harder than the rest of my peers. I am a living example of that if you work hard towards your goal, you can become who you want to be and lead a better life than the lives of your father and mother and become who you would want to become. I didn't let my poverty-stricken background stop me from perusing my goal nor did I let what people think of me stop me from what my heart is telling me is the right thing to do. I refused to accept the notion that I couldn't do what I was planning to do because I was a poor child from a poor parent. Instead, I embraced the facts that I was poor and my parents were completely poor, and I became proud of it and that became the norm to me so it did not bother me at school or when I am socializing with my teenage friends walking with them in that torn clothes of mine, and walking barefoot with no shoes on my feet, while they wore good clothes and shoes or walking bare-chested because I didn't have a shirt or to put on or worn or dirty shorts because I couldn't afford soap to wash the only shorts and the shirts I have.

Sometimes, I was embarrassed when I came across a good-looking girl and I always wondered what they were thinking about me because my poverty was evident in what I was wearing. I sometimes became insecure and wanted to hide, but at the same time, I knew that if I don't socialize with people, I would lag behind and not gain the knowledge. I needed to face this tough world, and it was because of that determination, courage, and perseverance that I was able to pick myself up when I was down.

I began to see things positively and to assure myself that things happen this way for a reason. I didn't choose to be born in poverty or to parents who were poor and started to think that there must be a reason and one reason I considered was that God wanted me to learn the experience growing up in poverty and that lesson was to better myself and the people around me. The other choice I had was simply to accept that I was poor and do nothing about it, like my friends who mostly ended up leading difficult lives of alcoholism and marriage before the age of fifteen and having children they couldn't afford to take care of, and who were then caught in poverty themselves.

I am proud of the decision I took at an early age to get out of poverty and do something about it. If all the poor children can take their futures in hand by giving them an education to open their eyes at an early age as I did to myself, I think the world would be a better place to live in. When I go back home to my village and see the children in my community without education, it breaks my heart. I always shed tears because I know that if these children could learn, they would be able to improve their lives and the lives of their parents and the lives of the people living in their community, but because of lack of support from the government and the community leaders, these young precious lives would be wasted because there is no one to give them guidance in life.

Growing up in total poverty taught me lifelong lessons, one is to appreciate everything I have in my life and give thanks to God every day for the good and the bad things I come across ,and another lesson I learned was to be more patient that things may not work faster than you might expect because you are beginning from scratch, and it takes longer for things to come together for you and also to be able to accept your failure as it comes your way and to dust yourself and move on.

I also learned to forgive myself when I did not succeed in the areas I wanted or the goals that I had set for myself to achieve for that year, and I also learned that I should forgive the people around me for the wrong that they might have done for me and with that forgiveness gave me the strength and ability to think even harder to overcome those challenges that were before me trying to derail my ambitious ability to acquire the knowledge through education. I also learn that life is full of challenges. It's not as a smooth ride as one would think but there are lots and lots of temptations that could derail one's ability to achieve a plan for a better future, I learn that when those temptations come your way one should know how to deal with it one at the time until all that is standing your way are cleared and you will begin to move on.

I also learned that one needs a support system in place, especially those loved ones who love you no matter what. The ones who will stand shoulder to shoulder with you in difficult times and good times, the one who will cry with you and mourn with you when you mourn or cry, the ones who stand by you and tell you it's okay to fail and encourages you to get up from your fall and dust up yourself and move on with your dreams, the one who will lift you up and dust you off when you fall.

It is the parent who will be by your side and encourage you all the way that you can do it and never to give up. The parent that will commend you for trying when you fail and tell your son and daughter, I know you can do it go back out there and kick some ass. I accepted failure most of the time and move on with my life, but as I move on there is always a lesson I learn from my failure, and I always make sure I tried to correct those failures and do better if I come to a similar situation, but as a son of a poor parent, it's always hard to move on when you fail to achieve the expected goal set for yourself because constantly you will be thinking that you have let my parents down, and I have caused more pain to their misery, which they have a lot to deal with in their life and you would not want to be that child that continued to cause pain in the life of your parents as you are the only hope for a better life.

I always wondered what my parents thought of me when I failed to meet that expectation because they never complained to me about that. They had unconditional love for me. They supported me when things did not go the way I was expecting. They were my first line of defense when I needed support. They were the first people I turned to when I was sad. They would say, "Son, look the world is a tough place to be in there will always be trials in your life and those trials will make you a better person so move on and do not give up your aspirations," and I listened to them and accepted my failure and started again down new path bigger goals and ambitions as to what I wanted to be in this earthly life.

I also learned empathy along the way. In my experience, without empathy, I was not going to be able to learn what I need to do to get to where I was able to learn where other people are coming from when we disagree on something and to be able to know their feelings both emotionally and physically. That helped me a lot as a person because I was able to learn from them and know that sometimes people do things with no intent to hurt someone's feelings but just to get the other person's point of view, but in the end, wind up hurting that person's feeling. Everything depends on how the person who receives the message interpreted the situation, so I am the first person to learn to move on quickly when I got my feelings hurt.

I am always quick to forgive myself first if I did something unintended that hurt someone, but should it turn out to hurt that person's feelings, I start by forgiving myself first and then ask for forgiveness from the person I have hurt their feelings. This allows me to open my heart and to know that we are all human beings, and we are all liable to make mistakes now and then and to understand that we are human and capable of making mistakes that can hurt people's feelings. I was able to think of myself as a human who can make decisions that will sometimes make people unhappy and that became the way I have overcome the laughing, discouragement, unpleasant comments I heard from people I came across on my quest for my journey to achieve a better life.

People would always put me down because I came from Adwila, from such a poor background where no one had ever been to college or achieved any greatness, but I have, from time to time, proven my critique wrong when achieved the goals I set for myself. I always thought differently from my detractors. The more criticism I got from my detractors, the more I was motivated to prove them wrong. Their negative thinking or assumptions only encouraged me to work harder and harder to achieve my goals. Any wrong they did toward me, I considered a blessing, inspiring me to achieve my goals, and I gave thanks that I learned from my parents such magnificent lessons about life from my beautiful, poor, uneducated parents of mine that we are all human and that we are all capable of making mistakes. But when we make those mistakes, we should ask these questions are we willing to accept the responsibility because of our mistake and use it to uplift one another or to better the life of another because you would not want to make those mistakes again and caused pain to one another.

Never again give up on what you want to do with your life. No one will make life better for you without you working hard for it, every child in a poor community needs someone to guide them and be there for them and tell them they can be somebody. Every poor child needs someone to motivate them and validate them, but above all, every poor child in the community wherever they are needs unconditional love and support from their parents and their caregivers. Every poor child needs guidance from both of their parents. The mother and father play a very important role in the child's development. Every child wants to see their mother and father live happily together.

I was that lucky child growing up with my father and mother by my side, all the suffering and starvation always went away when I saw both my parents were together. It became an assurance to me that everything will be okay because my father and mother would take care of what may not be going well in my life. I like to use this analogy for my mother and father. My father was that lonely pole that supports a grass thatch house where many support branches grow, and the pole makes sure all those small branches are protected and grow up healthy, and my mother was the roof of the grass thatch house that covered all of us under her roof to make sure we were all protected, fed, housed, clothed, and made sure we were all healthy. Mom performed that role to the best of her ability by doing what she could with what little she had.

Mom took her role as mother very seriously. She nurtured us all very well. She was a compassionate woman who cared for all in our community, and she did not want to see anybody go hungry or thirsty in the village. That sense of community helped us a lot because we saw humanity in all people and with humanity in our hearts. I was able to see the world in different ways. First, I was able to accept that I was born in a poor family and that I would have to work harder if I want to succeed in all areas of life and that acceptance has made me more open to other people who will be willing to share their experiences so that I can better my life and the lives of my family.

I was able to listen to people many ideas and try to internalize these ideas in my heart, and the good ideas I tried to emulate the good ideas and used my negative experiences to avoid making mistakes. Life was not always been easy for me and my family. Sometimes, I felt I should give up in the pursuit of a better life but seeing my parents and siblings with no good clothes s to wear motivated me and to do something to get my family the better life they needed desperately.

I didn't want to be seen by my parents as the person who let them down and to see myself as a failure because that was not what I wanted to associate myself with. I was determined to work hard towards achieving all my goals of a better life for myself and my family, and nothing was going to stop me from that. It was a difficult and long road to travel, but I refused to accept the fact that I may not succeed in achieving my goals. I came to learn from my failures, and they became lessons for me because every step of the way I was met with failures, and from them, I always learned a new lesson about moving on and avoided making similar mistakes. I also learned that society can be very harsh and mean towards people who fall short of their goals. Instead of sending the message that it's okay to fail to achieve your intended goals in life, and not to let failure stop you from the pursuing what you want to achieve in your life.

Society must do a better job in encouraging those who are left behind, be it in education, employment, economic success, whatever form it takes. Let's support our neighbors, friends, strangers, brothers, and sisters and let them know that one should not let that failure stop them from getting back up and learning from their failure and moving on and aiming for greatness in life. My faith, courage, and determination guided me through my struggle for a better life, faith made me believe I can do whatever I want to do, and God is always by my side, watching and guiding me. Believing that I can meet my goals has ever crossed my mind, the belief that I was destined for greatness gave me the strength to wake up every day and thank God for allowing me to get up this morning healthy. Please continue to guide me in all I am doing to better my life and the lives of my family. Please don't let me disappoint my parents and allow me to continue to do things that are pleasing in your eyes and help me avoid doing things that are not pleasing in your eyes.

I believed as a child that faith in God will lead me to greatness, and I thank my parents for instilling that in me. Trust in God is my top value in life, I knew that without God I would be nothing and without trust in God, life would have no meaning for me. I knew that God had created me in this world for a higher purpose, and to achieve that purpose, I must believe in Him first and open my heart to him and surrender all my life to him. My mother and father taught me that God will always be on our side. In bad times or good, he would always be there for us and the fear of God was so strong in my heart that it made me think twice before making choices because I wanted to do things that are pleasing in the eyes of God. I didn't want to make my God angry with me.

The fear of God made us learn good from bad. When we were very young both my sisters and brother learned how to work together and love one another so that God will be happy with us. My parents taught all his children the power of forgiveness. When we did wrong to our brothers and sisters, these made us build such a strong family bond and values. We knew that in order to be a strong family, we should work together to achieve greatness, and whatever goals we hoped to achieve as a family. We all were striving to do good things that pleased our God, and I always wondered if we didn't have that direction, what would have happened to all of us or what would have happened to my eight sisters and my four brothers? Would we all be alive today? I would never know the answer to this question but what I know for sure God is alive and God will continue to be with me and my sisters and brothers for eternity and will continue to protect me and guide me in all my decision-making.

God has continued to bless me with good health and allowed me to do things that are pleasing in his eyes and doing the work to help the poor and the vulnerable people. I will always be grateful and appreciative for the value that my father and mother gave to us all his twelve children for the love of our God and to teach us to put God first in all that we do, and this powerful lesson has guided me all my life and will continue to be with me for the rest of my life on earth.

Courage and determination also played a big part in my quest for a better life. I was able to learn from my past mistakes and not let anyone stop me from trying to achieve the goals I set for my life. I refused to accept advice from people telling me I couldn't do something because it is not my area of expertise or I am not good at it, but, instead, I would go ahead and do it going against the will of the people that said couldn't do it because it is not my areas of expertise because I wanted to get the experience of doing something so that I could fail and learn why I came up short, and I would make sure I follow up with the project to learn what I can do to make it better. As a young man, I was the type of person you couldn't say no to. I would not accept a no as an answer. Instead, I was persistent in what I did. If you said no to me, I would not be satisfied with the answer. I would be inquisitive, wanting to know the reason or explanation for the rejection, because I wanted to learn from my mistakes so that when I come to that similar situation, I would get it right.

I always wonder to myself what has become of me today had I not worked so hard to be the person I am today. Without hard work and determination, courage, and listening to good advice from the people around me, would I have achieved my goals in life without listening to my father and mother's advice and teaching? All these thoughts, when I look back on them, led me to conclude that life is a journey full of highs and lows that need to be navigated carefully for one to succeed. Success requires collective thinking to acquire more knowledge to guide us to our path we choose to take.

It would be a long road but never give up on your goal for a better life for yourself and your family. Poverty and inequality are evils that stop poor people from achieving their goals, be they financial goals, housing goals, education goals, health goals, family goals, whichever goals you chose, journey poverty should not deter you from working hard to achieve your goals. Find someone you admire and resolve that you want to be like that person and let it sink in that you will do what it takes to be like that person but be ready to accept the failures along the way and be able to adjust yourself to accept those failures and learn from them and dust yourself and get back up again and start moving on.

Don't let poverty stop you from pursuing your goals, but for me, I knew that education was my only hope, and the question became how would I be able to achieve my goal of obtaining education, and I knew poverty was standing in my way of achieving that goal, but I refused to let poverty stop me from getting an education and I told myself I would do what it took to get my education. Poverty affected everyone's ability to think—the ability to concentrate on your work because you don't know where your next meal is coming from.

The ability to be happy as a child even though you didn't have a good night sleep because of lack of a mattress or clean bedsheets to cover yourself, the ability to think right when you are hungry, the lack of energy to play with your friends due to hunger because the little food your parents gave you every night couldn't sustain you the all day until the next meal in the evening, all these are challenges facing the poor. Poverty is the dreaded disease that affects all children in poor communities around the world. Poverty affected me in ways I will never forget. I always wondered if I had not grown in a home without abject poverty maybe I would have achieved more greatness in life than what I had. I always wonder had I have enough food to eat when I was young if I would've been able to, like playing sports like the other kids. I loved sports, but I didn't have the energy to play because I was hungry and didn't have the energy.

When I was a young boy, I loved to run a lot, and I wanted to be an athlete and a runner, but that dream came crashing down because of poverty. I couldn't run every day because I was weak and didn't have the necessary nutrition I needed to have the much-needed energy that would sustain me every day to be able to participate in sports, especially long-distance running, which required a lot of energy.

It has become clear to me that poverty prevented me to discover my true potential talent as a child growing up in rural northern Uganda. I was unable to discover my God-given potential because I was limited with resources due to poverty. I was unhappy because I was limited as to what I could and I couldn't do because of poverty, and that should not happen to any child in this world. Children are created by God to be happy and grow in a loving environment and discover their God-given potential talent and learn to contribute to society, but many millions of children around the world are still in this predicament with no way to get out of poverty, and this breaks my heart.

136

Today, poverty and inequality in poor communities around the world have created a big gap between haves and have-nots. Parents in my community couldn't afford to send their children to school because of a lack of money to pay for their education. The cost of living increased and made education very expensive for poor parents around the world. This is compounded by the problem of climate change, which is now affecting poor communities around the world. When I went back to Uganda to visit my family in Northern Uganda what I experienced and observed in my communities was quite alarming and different from when I was growing up because the land has become less fertile due to overuse, heavy rains caused by climate change have washed away topsoil and left it bare, which couldn't be cultivated for farming and crops that are planted are always washed away by the heavy rain. Prolonged drought caused by climate change dries up all the crops planted by farmers.

Families are poorer than when I was growing up because back then, we were able to grow our food, and excess food was sold to the market to pay for our education but now parents can't afford to do that due to climate change and other natural disasters that have caused more poverty and inequality to poor communities around the world because their crops in the garden are all destroyed by all these forces of climate change.

Children born into poor families have no chance to achieve greatness because they have not been given a chance to do so. I was touched to see many children in my community malnourished due to lack of proper food or no food at all and many not attending school because their parents could not afford to pay for their education and many girls are left to wait for marriage at a young age, just as it was when I was growing up. It breaks my heart to see Uganda going backward instead of moving forward. I see education as the key to obtain a better life for the poor children in poor communities in Uganda and other poor communities around the world as it was for me.

To all people in power, be it nonprofit or corporate executives, let's work together to answer the call to help the children born in poor communities. The time is now, and we should not wait for long since the gap between the poor and the rich has grown wider and wider. We should work together to close these gaps and help poor children around the world.

CHAPTER 11:
Returning to a Changed Community

~~~

C LIMATE CHANGE AROUND the world will cause catastrophic effects on poor people around the world die of starvation and disease caused by climate change will be great if nothing is done to address this changing world. People in the communities around the world would be forced to migrate to look for food and water to feed their children, and there would be conflict and wars within countries over natural resources and countries will not be able to protect their borders due to massive desperate populations who will be seeking food to feed their children. Water will be a rare commodity that the world population world will fight to control.

It makes me wonder what the poor countries will do to withstand the effects of climate change if the developed countries think climate change is a hoax created by politicians. After many years of living in the developed world, I went back home to the land and the country I loved so much. my mother country where I was born and raised, the land where I learned to walk and talk, the land full of natural beauty tall trees and tall grass, abundant with beautiful birds and wild animals, the cry of hyenas at night, the singing of crested crane birds, and the sight of different species of the beautiful birds fly over your head as a young man was magnificent to watch and love. There was a tall mango tree in the village. When they were hungry, the children of the village climbed the mango tree high up like monkeys and ate the ripe mangoes until their bellies were full of fruit juice and hunger was gone. Then we'd go home to wait for your parents to come back from long day tending the garden and prepare dinner for the entire family to eat.

The wild forest trees that produced fruit became the first line of defense for food security for children in our community in northern Uganda because families could not provide lunch and breakfast to their children in the morning and lunchtime, so searching for fruit became our breakfast and lunch, while we waited for our mom and father to come back from the garden and prepare for us much-needed dinner. Hunting for wild animals to supplement our diets was fun, learning the skills our father and other family members in the community used to trap the wild birds and wild animals to supplement our diet made life living in the village interesting, despite our poverty.

The experience of hiding under the tall grass and trees and play with other children was fun and exciting and made life despite having no video games or football to play like in the developed world. My trip back home in 2015 opened my eyes to my worst fears about what would happen to my childhood community when the land they depend on their land disappeared or became inhabitable and could no longer sustain life or feed the entire population living in our communities. The answers to these four questions became a reality to me, the fear I had forty years ago for my community had returned and needed to be dealt with head-on. In my former village, there are no more tall trees or the tall grass I grew up with.

The land had become bare, and soil erosion was the cause. In any slight rain, you see how the topsoil is being washed away by the running water. The dry season is extremely very hot with lots of wildfires. Food insecurity is rampant, and families can't afford to feed their children since they live in abject poverty. Many children and their families are malnourished due to the lack of a proper diet. The wild animals and birds that we used to hunt to supplement our diet when I was growing up are all gone now. The beautiful birds that used to sing at night and woke us up are all gone. The wild animals that used to live alongside our homes are all gone. Climate change has stripped them away.

The natural beauty of our landscape is defenseless, and it's just a matter of time when there will be no life left in our villages. If nothing is urgently done to reverse the effect of climate change in my community, other communities around Uganda, and communities around the world facing a similar situation. Poverty and climate change is a bad combination because poor people will have no other alternative to turn to feed their children except to cut down trees to create land to plant crops to feed their children, cutting trees down to burn into charcoal as a form of energy to cook food for their children leaving the land they desperately need to plant crop to feed their children bare, which is therefore susceptible to soil erosion when it rains. Heavy rain in the village is washing away topsoil, which contains soil nutrients that the plant crops needed for growth this is causing big problems for the poor community in the Lira district, in which my community is located, soil erosion, and mudslides are the cause of the day leading to the death to many innocent poor families in Uganda living in most of these affected areas.

The land is bare now which cannot sustain the wild animals, their habitat is now completely destroyed the beautiful birds and beautiful wild animals I grew up watching are now all wiped out, which really breaks my heart because the young children growing up now will not have the opportunity of having fun of watching wild birds and wild animals in their neighborhood in their natural habitats. The birds singing and flying around and over the roof over our house are gone and this broke my heart, and I hope we all will do our part to help the poor community overcome this life and death situation that climate change is having a devastating effect on the poor community where they do not know where to turn to feed their children. When we were growing up in Northern Uganda in a poverty-stricken community with my mother and father and my eleven siblings, I had hopes and dreams that one day things would be okay if we worked hard and did the right things.

The reasons I was so optimistic was that we had very fertile land to grow our crops, which were enough to feed all of us in our household, and the surplus we sold to the market to help us buy essential goods like soap, salt, clothes, pay for medical care for our family, pay for our education school fees, but now with the effect of climate change my community are now left with little or nothing to work with because the precious resources that everyone relies on are now rendered valueless, because the land is no longer fertile to produce enough food to feed their children in the community they live.

Very little food is being produced that couldn't sustain the entire family until the next season for another harvest, and as a result, many families in our community every year are facing starvation as result of climate change. Many families in our community cannot afford to send their children to school because education has become too expensive for the people in rural communities since they do not even have enough food to feed their children, and this is causing devastation in our community.

Young people had no dreams and hopes in life like I did when growing up, they see nowhere to turn to for help and, as a result, many have turned to alcohol abuse and early marriages for both young men and young girls. Many are dropping out of primary and secondary school because their parents can't afford secondary school and high school, and this is making life in my community and the community around Uganda desperate because early marriages mean having children at the age of twelve and fifteen years old, increasing the population in the community, which is already strained for resources due to climate change, and fewer resources are available to accommodate the increase in the population. The land is incapable of absorbing the increase in population in Northern Uganda. Unless something is drastically done to change the trend, the result will be death in many communities in Uganda because the existing resources now can't meet the increase in population and many children will die due to lack of nutrition.

Food insecurity is now rampant because the land has become infertile due to over-cultivation and the cutting down of trees that support the ecosystem, and the rainfall pattern has changed because of climate change. Soil erosion has become rampant, and mudslides have caused many deaths around Uganda, and I fear that if nothing is done soon to address this manmade disaster many more lives will be lost. Poverty never stopped me from pursuing my dreams. I worked so hard with my mother and father in the cotton garden, sweet potatoes garden and onion garden, beans gardens, maize garden, cabbage garden, and cassava garden to grow all these crops to support our family with much-needed food and the rest my father and my mother sell it to get money to pay for our school fees for our education and my siblings, and I was grateful to our parents for teaching us the value of hard work at an early age to fend for ourselves and to be to help our community with the little food we grow, and we thanked our father and mother that constant reminder to us all the siblings that all will be okay if we work hard and trust God and put Him first in all what we do and because of that it opens my mind to see the world from a different perspective.

Even though I grew up in a family in abject poverty, I was able to comfort myself and my heart and soul that things will be better one day for myself and my family. My father and mother gave us strength to live and the reasons to keep hopes and dreams alive that one day I and my siblings will be okay and will come out of poverty and lead a better life than them if only we work hard for it because we were coming from a very poor and poverty-stricken family and the community, and I am glad and proud that I listened to the advice of my mother and father without them. I don't know where I would be now most likely I would have been dead by now like many of my colleagues who were not so lucky and took a wrong path in their life and ended up dead. I am afraid that many children in my community have lost the hope and the dreams I had when I was growing up because they see no opportunity for them in their future in this world because the only resources their father and mother have is the land that has become unproductive and not fertile at all and is not producing enough food for their consumption and to feed their children.

The situation is made worse by climate change and because of that many children are resulting in early pregnancy and early marriages. And many families in my communities have no means or resources to adapt to modern technology in farming because this technology requires lots of money to acquire. People in most rural Ugandan communities lived on near-zero income and can't even afford to buy simple things like salt and soap for their families. It's impossible to talk to the people in these communities about acquiring the modern technology tools to help them improve on their agricultural output unless the government is willing to assist the poor communities to acquire it and to teach the poor people in the communities around the country the importance of using modern technology to improve the farming in Uganda and must be free for all the poor communities around the country of Uganda.

Also, the government should invest in young people by providing free education to poor children in the communities up to college, and many of these young people coming from poor communities around the countries will be encouraged to take courses involving farming as agriculture is the backbone of Uganda economy, and it's the only areas with jobs opportunities available around the country so that when this young men and women graduate they will go back to their communities and create jobs for themselves and people in their communities, and they will teach their communities the importance of acquiring modern technology in agriculture to produce enough food for their families, and the excess can be sold to the market to provide them income to support their families in other areas, like paying for education for their children and paying for medical care for themselves and their love ones. Also, the extra income will be used to buy essential items like clothes, soap, salt, medicine for their families, and I believe this will reduce the suffering of the poor communities around the country. Agriculture employs many poor populations in Uganda, and it's the only area of the Uganda economy that, in my opinion, the government must invest on it heavily to help the majority population employ in these areas to lift them and their family out of poverty. I am the living proof that without agriculture, I would not be where I am today if not because of farming. My family worked hard in the cotton fields and other crops and vegetable planting to allow my mother and father to earn money to pay for my education and education for my sisters and brothers and take care of our family.

Climate change is a threat to humankind in the world especially in poor countries in Africa where people depend on agriculture for their livelihood, the world must come together to address this crisis of climate change. When I went back home in Uganda to my home village in Lira where I was born and raised on the land which was fertile enough to produce us much needed food to feed us all in the family. I was shocked to see the barren land that remained of my formerly lush community. As a result of climate change, rainfall is no longer reliable to help farmers in my community to farm the crop to feed their children, flooding has become a way of life in many parts of Uganda whereby people's houses are swept away as a result of heavy rainfall. Landslides have become part of the norm in many parts of Uganda, killing many people. The land has become so dry with an increase in temperature drying a lot of agriculture, making it difficult to grow crops because the temperature is so high as to dry up all the crop planted with many trees cut down by poor community to provide them with a source of fuel to generate energy for cooking food, leaving lands bare suspectable to soil erosion, and with an increased percentage of the population in the community, with limited resources to feed the increase in the population the little resources is now being shared with the increased number in the population increasing more stress in the community and the climate.

The world must pay attention to the increased number of populations in poor countries especially in Africa where climate change is threatening the survival of the human population and livestock. Water has become a problem to the communities because the natural springs are drying up, leaving communities across the continent of Africa with limited water for drinking. When I was growing up in rural northern Uganda, we had numerous swells all over our communities where many children in the communities go and draw clean drinking water for home use and for animals to drink, but to my surprise, when I went back home, I found that many of those wells and springs that I grew up with all are now dried up, and people have nowhere to go and fetch the water from but to walk long distances to go and look for clean drinking water for both their animals and for home consumption.

Climate change will destroy all the poor countries if nothing is done to change the trajectory of how poor countries in Africa can be helped to revise this alarming trend. When I think about climate, I think about the poor malnourished children in my community who have nothing to eat but to depend on their poor parents working hard to gather food in the wilderness to come and feed their children and because climate change is now changing all the way they live. At the same time, they don't have the means to cope with climate change for survival because all their livelihood depends on land and because they don't have the resources or the financial capital to help them change their ways of life to according to climate change. I am worried if nothing is done to change the trajectory on time of this killer called climate change poor communities around the world will be wiped out and there will be no living creatures living in poor countries around the world.

The people of the world must not turn their back to the poor population around the world because we are all human being created in God's image and deserve to live in this beautiful world with love and dignity, and I am grateful, and I will always be grateful to my mother and father for working tirelessly day and night to make sure we have enough food to eat and drink under very difficult circumstances. They did their best to try to provide for their twelve children the best they could under very hard conditions they were in, and I am proud of my parents for sacrificing all their lives to work hard to see all their twelve children grew up to be an adult and become mothers and fathers of their own. I am grateful that God gave them the heart and the brain to see human beings as God's children and them having that compassionate heart to care for each of them, regardless of whether they were their children or not. I am thankful for my mother and father for teaching their children the art of caring for one another and teaching us all to see other people as God's children and to love them as our own brother and sisters, and to be able to examine our hearts to make sure we hold the principle close all the times.

Mother and Father taught us the value of smiling. I remember when I was a young boy growing up I was eleven years old and I was coming back from school having walk several miles to and from school, and I was exhausted because we stayed all day at school without eating or drinking water, so I was both hungry and thirsty and exhausted, and

I needed something to eat badly that on my way back home, I wasn't talking to anybody, including my friends because I wanted to reserve the energy I had left with to get home to my mother and father and see if they've prepared something for dinner. We do not have lunch so we relied on eating fruits and roots for lunch to keep us fed until dinner in the evening.

I remember that day I had a lot on my mind, wondering why is it I have to go through this difficult time in my life, suffering with my mother and father who cannot afford to buy us the food and clothes we need while other children's parents had the ability to afford those essential things to their children. I was angry, and I wanted to get home and put those questions to my parents, so I was not smiling at all. I had that angry face on me when I got home and went straight to my mother as always, every day to see if she has prepared something for us to eat. Most of the time when we get back from school we would find her busy in the hut cooking full of smoke from firewood and she did not see our faces when we get home until when she finished cooking and serving food and called us to come and take the food out and put on the floor and gathered us to come eat.

But that day something happened when I got home from school. I found my mother had finished cooking, and she was sitting under the mango tree waiting for us to come back from school and eat the food that she had prepared for us. But on that day, I noticed my mother looking at me very closely straight in the eyes when I was approaching home, and when I was about to enter our grass thatch house build with mud and smeared beautifully with cow dung and black soil that makes it glitter, my mother was sitting on the veranda of her house watching all her children come back from school. When I was about to go inside, my mother called me and asked me to sit down near her and asked me how my day at school was and if there was something wrong that happened to me at school because she could tell on my face there was something wrong with me. I didn't have a happy face and was not smiling, and I was like in my heart how did she know that I was not happy? I was quiet for a while and not answer my mother's question, but I thought about it, and I wanted to tell her why, so I did what young people always do, and I asked her how did she know I wasn't happy? And she replied, "My son, I can tell from your face and your body language tells me so."

This provided the opportunity for my mother to teach me the importance of smiling all the time at the people we met. That day, my mother taught me that even if something is wrong, I should keep a smile on my face where no one will tell because whoever you are meeting or come in contact with is not the cause of your unhappiness and that person does not deserve to see your unhappy face, and by keeping on your happy and smiling face it will open for you the opportunities to talk and forget about what is troubling you. I am grateful that I had that lesson from my mother at such a young age the importance of smiling. I didn't know how important that lesson in my life growing up but when I became an adult, I realized how important that lesson of smiling my mother taught me would help open the doors for me, and I am proud of my illiterate mother and father for using their common sense values and instilling in me such an important lesson and values and allow me to apply it in my life at an early age. I was able to teach my own child the same values, and I hope my children will teach my grandchildren the same values and pass them on for the generations to come to make the world a better place to live with many people smiling and less finger-pointing. That is my hope.

My mother and father were good listeners. They listened to us all the time and made good decisions that benefitted them and me and my siblings. We learned from our father the importance of listening. Mom told her children she wanted us to listen very closely for what she wanted us to do for her before we did something, and we all followed her instructions very carefully. If she wanted us to do something for her and if you didn't listen carefully or follow the instructions as stated by her, you knew you would pay the price for not listening.

Mom and my father knew how to get us to listen to them and do the right things, the things they wanted done. My mother and father used calm, polite voices when communicating with us. So, when we didn't listen carefully, we could have easily missed what they are saying, so that motivated us to listen carefully and pay attention to what our parents were saying to us. Our parents never yelled at us, and I am glad they didn't because they gave us a valuable lesson as children that helped a lot when we grew up and had our own children, and we were able to instill the same value we learned from our father and mother to our children.

My parents had a compassionate heart and cared about everyone they met, they cared about their twelve children and the children in our village and children anywhere they come in contact with and that level of caring and having a compassionate heart. They showed to their children and the people they met a valuable lesson as their children to love and care for everyone we meet. Our mother and father taught us the value of opening our hearts to people around us and loving them the same way we love our brothers and sisters.

Our parents taught us what perseverance meant because we saw in them how they persevered during very difficult times, raising their twelve children in abject poverty. They were able to show us the way to use our power of choice to liberate us from the poverty we were in and the power of choice was the greatest tool we had to make a good decision for our future.

We had the choice to either continue to whine about our continued living in poverty or we could choose to do something meaningful with our lives that would lead us out of poverty and our illiterate father and mother's common sense told them the only solution was to send their children to school to acquire the knowledge that their own parents denied them, and Mother and Father did not want the repeat of what had happened to them to again happen to their own children, and they did not want history to judge them harshly. My parents were able to do their best to make sure we all attended school by selling their vegetables and working in cotton fields to raise money for our school fees. Our parents taught us the importance of not being afraid to ask for help if we needed to and that lesson stuck with me when I was growing up, and I didn't know it would work for me but it turned out to be the most important lesson I needed in my adult life: If I wanted to succeed in life I needed to ask for help and guidance from people I trusted to guide me step by step to overcome my obstacles.

Mother and Father were very happy people they can talk to any stranger they met on the road. As a young child, I would ask my parents, "Why do you have to talk to someone you don't know and ask them how they were doing?" which I saw as strange. However, as I got older and became a young man, I started to see the reason why my father and mother talked to strangers. I realized the reason why they were loved by the community around us and the same also went for the people my mother and father don't know. I realized that is the power and strength both my parents have to draw people to them and become good leaders in the community. They did that because they open their heart to the people around them by simply smiling and laughing with them and showing them that they cared about them and they did that by asking the strangers how they were doing and laughing with them.

This is one of the most powerful tools I learned from my father and mother. Having a positive attitude all the time and laughing and smiling all the time will help you through the day. Even if you are having a bad day and open the doors for you to meet good people that will help you on your way with professional growth, and I thank my mother and father for teaching me that valuable lesson that opened the doors for me and for teaching me why we should focus on things that matter most in our lives and things that will bring joy in my life and do away with things that bring bad energy to my life and because of this valuable lesson I learned from Mother and Father, I was able to focus on things that matter most in my life and stay away from things that will destroy my life, like avoiding the wrong groups, avoiding drinking alcohol, avoiding smoking cigarettes, and avoiding getting married at a young age when I was not ready to take care of my family and to associate with people I saw as good role models.

Mother and Father taught me that life can be unpredictable and that I should embrace it and use the lesson to better my goal set in life and not let it bring me down, my parents told me I will always stumble and fall in life, but when I do stumble, I should get up and dust myself off and move on and be able to turn negative criticism into a positive by learning from the experience. Mom and Father said I should refuse to accept the concept of what I can and cannot do.

Mother and Father told me I could do anything I want to do as long as it's what my heart wanted me to do, and I am grateful for them to let me explore my own journey in life without them deciding them deciding it for me and for that I thank them and I will always spread that same concept to my children and my grandchildren and the children around the world for parents around the world to let their children chose their own path in life with no any interference with their parents.

The greatest lesson I learned from my father and mother when I was twelve years old going for senior one in a secondary school, and I was leaving home to go to attend school at a boarding school [add school] where I will be staying at school with other young men from different part of Uganda, and my mother and father knew it was going to be a life challenge for me because I was coming from a very poor family with one good clothes and slippers, one bedsheet, no blanket, and one uniform in my suitcase. So, I didn't have a lot to take with me to help me at school like other parents may have provided for their children. I think that bothered my Mom and Father tremendously because they didn't want me to have a bad feeling when I reached the boarding school and see what other children that I didn't so I think they wanted to get ahead of it and let me know that all those things that other kids might have that I didn't matter. What mattered was only my education and because of that they gave me the most valuable lesson I would never forget for the rest of my life, and the lesson was, "Do not let your past rule your present."

My mother and father wanted me to focus on the present and not dwell on what had happened to me in the past because they knew it is not important and would not help me move forward with my life. My parents wanted me to accept my past and move forward because I can't change what had already happened to me or what I have gone through in the past but to work hard as much as possible to make sure my present became better and happier and to be able to better their life and the life of my sisters and brothers as well. My mother and my father knew there is nothing in my power I could do to change my past to what has happened to me when I was young. They knew it was not my choice to be born in a poor family, but it was God who gave them that gift of life of a child to be born in their poor family, and they were thankful that God gave them the precious gift of a baby boy.

Mother and Father wanted to protect me from the harm's way and from the forces around me, most importantly to protect me from the pain and the hard times I endured growing up as a young boy, walking miles and miles to take livestock in the wilderness looking for water to drink, the pain of waking up in the middle of the night to go to the garden to dig and plow the garden and help my mother and father before we can start a long journey to school, the pain of not having enough to eat and drink at home having worked for a long day in gardens with our mother and father, the pain of walking long distances to look for clean drinking water for our family, the pain of seeing other children wearing clean clothes and you cannot afford them is heart-breaking as a child growing up.

Mother and Father didn't want all this pain to stop me from pursuing my dreams and my parents didn't want my past to rule my life, and I am grateful that my mother and father were able to shield me from my darkest past and help me move forward with an open mind to focus on my present, not my past. I refused to think about what I went through as a child growing up in a poverty-stricken home with my mother and father, and I didn't want my life to be defined by my past but I wanted my past to be a success story that will help the millions of children around the world who are faced with the similar life story to mine to let them know there is hope for them to have a better life if they work hard together with their parents and listen to their parents advise and doing the right thing all the time and setting high standards which they will start working toward achieving those goals.

Perseverance has helped me built the strength I needed to face the life-challenging situations in my life. It has made me stronger to face any adversity in my life. It has given me courage in doing things one would say it's impossible to do. It has made me be honest about myself in all that I do for myself and others, with bravery I persevered during those hard times. In my life, I can tackle things in a more just way because I do not want to cause pain and suffering in people's hearts because I know what the pains feel like because I went through those pains in my life. Growing in poverty and suffering has conditioned me to appreciate all the little things I have to achieve in my life, most importantly it has built me to have the courage to confront my weakness and find ways and means to improve on those areas of weakness. It has allowed me to challenge myself and go above and beyond out of my comfort zone to try things that make people feel uncomfortable by asking direct questions to people that will sometimes make them uncomfortable but getting honest feedback answer from people helps me learn and be a better person and a better leader.

By keeping hope in my heart all the time it has helped me manage stress and anxiety and cope with adversity, hope in my heart kept me going with life and feel good about myself and be happy and not think about what I was going through but to concentrate on my goal of getting my education and building a better life for myself and my family. Hope gave me the courage and ability and comfort and the feeling that all will be okay no matter how difficult what I was going through in my life, the ability to think that things will be okay if I work hard for it is so comforting in my mind and the knowledge gave assured me that whatever I was working on to achieve in my life was going to succeed and the feeling made me work hard to achieve my goals set.

I never gave up hope in my life. I held hope close in my heart and never let it go because I knew it was the most important tool, I had to help steer me in the right direction in my life. I never wanted to go to the situation of the feeling of hopelessness when facing difficulty and when I come around to a situation that would put me in a situation of feeling hopeless. I will make sure hope guides my thinking and try to avoid the thinking of hopelessness. Hope in my heart gave me an opportunity made me show appreciation to all I met and to all who helped me in the cause of my struggle to get my education in order to have a better life without hope in my heart I don't think I was going to show my appreciation to all who worked with me to achieve greatness for myself and my family.

Hope in my heart gave me the ability to care for and love others.

It gave me the ability to listen to the people in my community and feel their pain as my own and coming together and sharing the pain in our hearts gave us the strength and courage we needed to tackle any problems that came our way. Hope gave me the courage to find passion in what I wanted to achieve in life and let my mind focus on my goals. Hope made me feel there was nothing I couldn't do. Hope built my heart with no fear to tackle anything that comes my way that will be useful to achieve my set goals. I remained hopeful that everything would be okay if I worked hard for it. Hope became a driving engine in my heart, I made hope part of my life and I know without hope in my heart I am nobody. I was able to overcome the trials and tribulations in my life with hope glued in my heart. I saw all the challenges that come before me as a test to my life to learn from them and be a better person and move on. I was always hopeful about what life challenges brought before me and I always look to those life challenges as a learning curve for me to achieve greatness in life. Whatever life challenges I faced, I handled them with grace and dignity and made sure they didn't put me down and if it does put me down, I have always figure out a way to get back up quickly to move on with my life.

CHAPTER 12:
Lessons Learned from Extraordinary Parents

L IFE BECOMES MEANINGLESS without hope. We have the courage to overcome any obstacle before us. I was able to soften my heart in all that I did and was confronted with because of hope, be it working with difficult people or accepting criticism with pride and a positive attitude because I wanted to learn as much as possible and gain as much knowledge as possible from the people I meet to open my future with limitless possibilities. Hope made me see things differently and think positively all the time, that there will be a better tomorrow regardless of what happened to me or what was happening to me, going hungry with no food to eat for myself, in which I can't afford good food to eat for my family I was, and always remain, hopeful. Hope has healed wounds in my heart because it made me see the world in a different way, that everyone born in this world has to face difficulty one way or another in their lifetime but when you face those challenges how you handle it to overcome those challenges and becomes a better person is the most important lesson. Hope teaches us all to become better people in life and face our challenges in life with pride with no same. When I was growing up in northern Uganda in total poverty with no clean drinking water, no electricity, no clean clothes or shoes to wear, walking barefoot to school ten miles away from my home with no breakfast or lunch to eat at school, hungry and exhausted all the time because I had not eaten enough food to keep me going, but I refused those challenges to define who I am, but hope gave me the opportunity that there will be a better tomorrow for me and my family.

I held the hope very close to my heart and I know from the beginning of my life that I should put hope at the center of all that I do and to trust the supernatural power from above, which is God, to guide me all that I do and to ask him forgiveness if I have done wrong to anyone I have come across. Hope and forgiveness are powerful tools in our hearts that lead us all to lead a better life. If you have opened your heart and practice forgiveness always, this will allow your heart and soul to heal and improve your general well-being because you will not be able to hold any toxicity in your heart if someone wrongs you.

Forgiveness heals your heart from all those toxic thoughts, which should have had adverse negative consequences in your life because you forgave the person who has done wrong to you and you will not be carrying excess baggage with you and for that reason, you will have a clear mind to do what matters most in life. By doing so you will always achieve your goals, and hope will always keep you believing that there is going to be a better tomorrow no matter what happens. My mother and father gave me hope. They taught me there would always be a tough road along the way in life, but I should always be hopeful that a better life is always ahead of me.

As a young child growing up in poverty in rural Uganda, my mother and father knew there is nothing much they could do to change our situation of being poor but what they did know for sure is to instill in their twelve children to believe there will be a better tomorrow for all of us if we work hard and believe in ourselves. And they did this by making sure that every evening during our fireplace gatherings our mother and father would ask us all how our day went and if there was something wrong that happened that they could help with.

That fireplace became the most important place for us to learn from our father and mother because they were able to communicate to us all in a way that made us all fall in love with our parents. Every day, our father and mother reminded us all that we are very poor and that they couldn't afford to buy us all that we want or need. At the same time, they would encourage us all that we should not let our poverty stop us from pursuing whatever dream we want to pursue in life because as young children there is nothing impossible that we couldn't do. They also reminded us that we needed to work hard because we lacked resources to aid us like other children of parents who had the means to pay for their children's schooling.

Our father and mother stood with us through our difficult times. They cried with us when the going was rough and we children thought we would not survive, but they assured us that all will be fine, that we should all believe in one another and help one another and lift one another when they fall, and that when we fall, we should all fall together and cry together and plan to get back up also must be together, after a while of doing things together with my brothers and sisters, I realized that our parents had set a theme for us to work together in all what we plan to do, and I began to realize the strength that comes from working together with my sisters and brothers.

I realized we are there for one another no matter what life challenges brought upon us, and when I was in college, I kept thinking to myself how someone who had no formal education could have such a brilliant plan and ideals and ideas to instill in their children the importance of working together to achieve a greater good for the future of their children for the betterment of their community and the world. I became interested as a young man growing up in poverty to know from my parents why they think it was important for us as children to learn and continue to work together if at all we want to achieve the greater good for us, and I began to ask several questions to my father and mother just to get an idea on how their thinking was with the hope I will be able to learn from them how they acquire their knowledge and apply it to their children.

The first thing that I learned from both of my parents was that they were very good listeners, and they paid a lot of attention to their children, and they asked good questions. They'd want to know why we wanted to know what we were asking about and what we would with the knowledge we received. As a young man growing up, I wanted to learn as much as possible to learn from my parents because it was fun to be around them. As a young child growing up, you need a parent who has an open mind, who is nonjudgmental, and who pays attention to what you're asking them. Both my parents had an open-minded approach. Any of us approach them without have of us and to all who met them. The other critical piece that I learned from my parents was the importance of working together as a team was the fact that they grew up in tribal group and worked together as a community to resolve the issue or matter pertaining to their community and within our Langi tribe, children were raised by the village and children were disciplined by community members. One child was everyone's child.

That sense of community was essential to shape the life of my parents and they learned a lot from their community, and they wanted to translate that to raising their own children the way they were brought up in the Langi tribe. When my Mother and Father were growing up, they were attacked by clan members of another, so by parents' community had to work as a team to defend their territory and protect their community from being attacked so it was very critical for the community members to work together pertaining to challenges facing their community, including being an attacked by other tribes, cattle rusting, or cattle raids by other tribes, so working together as a team was paramount. Father and Mother's community had formed a collective in which they worked together to farm the land, plowing, sowing, and planting their seeds in the garden they owned. The work was done in groups of ten to fifteen people to increase the manpower to plow larger gardens to be able to obtain high yields to feed their children and the rest to feed their village's children.

As a young child growing in the community of the Langi tribe and observing and learning how the community came together and worked together in the field and shared what little that they had with their community members. Then, I came to realize where my mother and father learned the importance of working together to achieve a higher purpose. My mother and father learned early in life the importance of togetherness. They knew the power of working together and the impact that made. They knew by working with one another that they became stronger to achieve any task or goals before them, so it was very important for them to make sure that the continuity they learned from their community continues with their children, and it was very important to my father and mother that they play that role well so that their children succeed into the future. I am glad that they instilled that in us. My Father and Mother loved to bring people together in the community and entertain many in their thatched grass hut and feed them and have drinks with them with their local brew made of our local millet and maize and cassava. Everyone in our community loved my mother and father for having such a strong sense of community to bring everyone together and enjoy the company of one another and plan for the future of their community and the children growing up in their community.

The community gathering at our home was one of the best experiences I enjoyed growing up. It helped me learned a lot from my community elders about what kind of life I wanted for myself and the life of my children when I grew up. I was able to learn the good and the bad and separate the bad and take the good at my heart, and I wanted to do something to change the bad when I grew up, and I came to realize that I can only be able to change that with the knowledge that I will acquire from educating myself by going to college and returning to my community to help change the bad areas which I saw when growing up in my community.

One of the areas that I was not okay with was the early marriage of young girls to older men. Older Fathers opted to let their young girls into marriage to men who could not even support their daughters financially but because of the greed of having cows to relieve their poverty and to provide means of plowing in the garden. Witnessing how they auctioned their daughters to the highest bidder was shocking and traumatizing, and I wanted to acquire knowledge through education to have a voice and come back to my community and say this practice of selling young girls through marriage by paying the bride price to the parent should stop because I witnessed it happening to all the girls I grew up with in my community.

Their parents did not send them to school, or if they did send them, they only did so until they reached the age of twelve or thirteen. In their minds, that was the time to stop the girls from going to school and to wait for the men to come and marry them so that they can collect the highest bride price that will be paid to the father and the mother of the young girls and the little young girl will be sold to that man regardless of the age difference. To me, this was not okay, but I was a young man with no say to my elders about how what they were doing was wrong and that they should stop because I feared I will be disowned in the village and be cast out as a young man who did not respect the elderly in the community. So, I was scared to death, even if I was seeing what was being done by our elders in the community as not being right, but I did not have the voice and power to stop it.

I knew education was the only means I had at my disposal to acquire the knowledge with the hope that in the future it will help me to stand up to the elders to stop what I call the barbaric behavior and the arms fathers and mothers in my community were inflicting to their beloved daughters, and I cannot just stand there and do nothing to stop the pain of very many young girls in my community that their mothers and fathers were imposing in them. I wanted the practice of paying a bride price to mothers and fathers for young girls to stop. My mother and father were big supporters of girls going to school and getting their education. She wanted the pain she went through as a young child with her own father for refusing to pay for her education not to happen to any girls in her community, but she could only do so much because the voices of the men in our community overpowered her voice as a woman. Back then, women's voices weren't honored because of their gender.

I saw with my own eyes how my own mother's voice was silenced by men in my community. That broke my heart as a young boy to see a strong woman standing up for young girls in her community and being treated the way she was treated. It was gut-wrenching for me, but I could not do anything to change the situation and protect my mother from those angry men. My mother was a strong woman who stood up bullies in my village, but because it was her alone and her voice alone, men just overlooked what she was saying to them regarding sending their daughters to school. After my mother confronted them on the issue of sending their girls to school, she was not taken seriously on her stand for girls' education in our community.

My mother stood up for her eight girls' education with our father. My father did not want to send the girls to school, and his reason was that he did not have money to pay the school fees for their eight daughters' education, which was valid because we were so very poor, and father could not afford to pay for the school fees for all twelve of us. But our mother stood up for her girls and told our father that if they cannot afford the school fees for the girls, then the boys will also remain home, but if they have to struggle to pay for education it would be for both the girls and the boys. My mother knew it was going to be a difficult road for her husband and her to come up with the school fees for twelve children, but she wanted her girls to attend school the education that his own father denied her. My parents struggled to send all their twelve children to school. But the struggle was too much for both of them to bear so when the girls completed primary seventh-grade education, they decided they could not afford to continue to pay for the education for the girls because the school fees at the secondary level became too expensive for them to afford, so with heavy heart, my mother's quest for education for her girls came to a close.

As young a man at that time, I could see the pain in my mother's eyes. She wanted the best for her girls, and she wanted her girls to attained the higher level of education that her own father denied her from, but, unfortunately, both could not reach that level to afford to pay for the education past primary level education because the little food they produced could not sustain the family for both food and for sale to obtain money to pay for their twelve children's education so they decided the girls' education would stop at primary seven, and that was the saddest day for my mother and father because they wanted the best for their girls but there was nothing they could do within their power. They did their best, but it was time to let it go and only four boys could continue with their education. My sisters became my heroes and continue to be my heroes until my last day on earth because they sacrificed their lives for their brothers to continue with their education.

I remember how loudly my younger sister cried to my mother as she begged to continue her education. I remember putting my arms around her shoulders and told her things will be okay, and she should not worry much God will look upon her with mercy, and she would have a better life without having an education, and I could not stop her from crying. She was hurt, and there was nothing anyone could do to stop her from crying. Her emotions were very high at that moment I wanted to make sure I read so hard to help our family from poverty because I knew it was because of poverty, which has prevented my mother and father to allow my bright sisters to continue with their schooling.

Poverty denied my sister way to discover their God-given talents to help better our community and the world around them and because of that, I wanted to work so hard to make sure I get rid of this evil called poverty that has denied my people so many avenues to excel and have a productive life and compete with our peers. Education became everything to me because I saw no other way out to obtain better life without education. I knew I would not obtain happiness for myself and my family and my community without it. I knew that without education there was no way I was going to help these incredible two people who had given birth to me and raised and wanted to pay back to them what I owe them for them sacrificing their lives for me and my sisters, and I wanted to have an education to one day make them proud for me and to bring smiles their faces that this evil called poverty had denied them for such a long time.

Education was my only escape from misery and suffering from my people and it provided me hope that console my soul that all will be fine one day and with that comfort, I was able to promise my beloved mother that one day we would come out of this suffering caused by this evil called poverty, and I would be able to take care of her and my father and all of our family and the community as a whole and I remember the smiles on my mother face and that was enough confirmation to me as a child that my mother would be so proud of me if I fulfilled the goal I told her. I told my mother I would build her a permanent house with a sheet-iron rooftop and move her out of the grass thatch hut and create a permanent water source. Secondly, I told her I would make sure I will put her in my car one day and drive her around, and the third promise was to put her on a plane so she could see the inside of a plane. I fulfilled all my promises to my mother except the third promise to put my mother in the plane and see inside of a plane. Death robbed me before I could fly my mother around the world to see inside of an airplane God wanted my mother more than I did.

Death robbed me of the most special people in my life. My mother and father both will always be in my heart. Death spares no one. If death chose which people to take and who not to take, my mother and father would have been spared.

When I emigrated to the United States twenty years ago, I was unable to see my mother and father for fifteen years for many reason, including raising children and going to school, but when the time was ready to travel to go and see my beloved father and mother, and I was excited that I was going to go home and fulfill all the promises I made to my mother and my father and that we were going to have a big celebration to God for allowing me to achieve my goal of obtaining my education, which g both my parents and I thought It was going to be impossible given the barriers I faced.

I was excited to share with my mother what I have so far achieved in my new country called America, and I wanted to arrange to bring my mother to my new country America home to introduce her to my friends and show her my accomplishment in life and for her to see with her own eyes. The son she almost lost during delivery due to lack of medical care, the son she had to carry miles and miles to save his life, the son who was born with no clothes to cover him at the time of birth. I just wanted for us to meet to shed tears of joy of the many blessings that God has rewarded me because she prayed for me to make sure I succeeded in life, but unfortunately this was the time that God wanted her as much as I did.

Photo: Mothers, grandmothers, and my sisters in our community gathered to welcome me back and a celebration organized for their lost son during my last visit in Lira in northern Uganda.

Photo: These are children in Adwila giving me a farewell during my last visit in our community and thanking me for the support I am providing for their education.

Chapter 13

WHEN I STARTED my journey, I had prepared to go home from America to see my mother and Father which I have not seen and meet for fifteen years in Adwila—Lira, Uganda, I was excited but at the same time very nervous about what to expect but my heart was full of joy because I had a lot of things I wanted to share with my mother. I wanted to make sure the first thing when I get back home in the rural village of Adwila where I was born and raised to hug my mother tight and cry on her shoulders like a young child and thank her for what both of them, my mother and father, did to shape my life to work hard and to make me be able to see the inside of an airplane and come to the land of plenty America and have a wonderful life, which I thought it was impossible or out of reach to a child like me who had come from nothing completely.

When the day for me to take pane to fly back home drew closer and closer, I became very nervous because I did know what to expect because I was told my mother health condition was not good, so I kept praying every day and night for God not to take away the life of my mother before I can see her and say, "Thank you, Mother, for what you did for me." When the day came to board the plane to go and see my mother, who I had not seen in fifteen years, I prayed to God for the last time before I boarded the plane. That day had come to go and see my mother. Please give me courage and determination to meet with her and talk to her and hear her soft voice and her counsel and pray to

God please do not take her life away before I meet with her, and God heard my prayers I was able to land on Ugandan soil safe and sound.

It was the month of March the sun was very bright, and the grass was coming up because the rainy season had just begun, and the birds were singing on the tree and the clear blue moon was up in the sky. A very beautiful afternoon at Entebbe International Airport, the only international airport in Uganda. At the airport, I was welcomed by my brother-in-law who was so happy to meet with me and pick me up and drive me home to reunite with my sisters.

After our brief conversation and hugs and laughing, my mind was only on the condition of my mother, so before long I asked my brother-in-law on our way from the airport to home how my mother was doing, and my brother-in-law said with a straight face, "She is not doing well. So, I want you when you get home to be strong as a man, although I know it will be tough on you because of your close relationship with your mother. You are her favorite son, and this will be tough on both of you, but I know you have the will, and you will be strong meet with your mother and enjoy each other company, but what my brother did not know that by saying she is not doing very well had really put my spirit down, and I didn't know what to expect in terms of my mother's condition. I didn't know whether she would be able to recognize her son that she has not seen for fifteen years. My spirit was so down and didn't know what to do. My heart was pounding and racing, as though I had just finished a 100-meter race. I was breathing fast, and I could not wait to see my mother.

I wished I had the wings to fly very fast to see my mother, but unfortunately, I did not. I made sure my mother was well aware and informed that I was on my way from America to see her, and I was told she was overwhelmed with joy and happiness that I was coming to see her. I did not want to surprise my mother because I knew she was sick and I knew she loved me so very much, so I wanted to avoid anything that would trigger shock to her body so I made sure she was updated every step of the way where I was and how long it will take me to reach to where she was staying.

When I was five minutes away from our home where my mother

Chapter 13

was staying my heart pounded so hard, and I thought maybe I was going to have a heart attack but no only because I was so nervous I did not know what to expect inside when I finally come face to face to meet my mother and when the time came and I reached our compound I dropped the bag I was carrying and ran straight to where my mother was and held her tight for ten to twenty minutes crying like a kid on the shoulders of my mother. She too was crying tears of joy and sadness, and my mother kept saying to me in our Langi language, "Amari matek atina," which is loosely translated in English as "I love you so very much, my son," while wiping away tears from her eyes.

My mother was so weak and thin that I could not recognize her face. She had been a strong, tall black woman, but because of her sickness, she had lost a lot of her body weight, and I kept asking my sisters what had happened to my mother and had she been to the doctor, and, if so, what did the doctor said what was wrong with her. Nobody from my family could answer that question. So, immediately I began to arrange to take my mother to the hospital to find out what was wrong.

I had to find a car to hire to take my mother to the hospital. When we reached the hospital, there was no doctor to see my mother. I was told by the people in the hospital that if you don't bribe the workers at the hospital, nobody will come and attend to my mother because the staff and the nurses at the hospitals are underpaid and that the only way they can survive is through bribery. If you pay the bribe, then you will be put in front of the line to see the doctor, so when I learned the trick, I talked to one of the nurses to see how she can help to connect me with a doctor to attend to my mother, and I told her if she could do me that favor I will reward her and thank her so very much for her kindness and support, and she agreed to help me and began to process to get my mother seen by the doctor by taking her temperature and weight, and once my mother was completely processed, we were moved to a different room to wait to see the doctor, and there I had to sit and wait for eight straight hours without the doctors appearing to come and see my mother.

The day came and went, and we had to spend the night at the hospital without any help and seeing patients dying on the floor next to your patient without any help from the doctors and nurses was so depressing, but I had to stay strong because of my mother. The night came and went with no help from the doctors or nurses when the morning came, I became impatient because I didn't want my mother to suffer the same fate as the other patients who were dying on the floor without being seen, so I decided to remove my mother from that hospital and take my mother to a private clinic where she was attended to very quickly and the doctors who examined my mother and gave the name of the sickness that was disturbing my mother. She was diagnosed with pancreatic cancer and given one month to live.

I just fell on the floor in another room and cried because there was nothing I could do, so I had only one month to be with my mother, someone I had not seen for fifteen years. Now, I had only one month or less to love my mother unconditionally and share all the memories we had within the limited days of her life in this world, so I wanted to be with my mother and hear from her what she really wanted to convey to me so that I could learn from her as much as possible. I could for the last time that I will be with her in this world because the time and the hour and days had now come close for my mother to leave and depart this world. Now, I came a realization that my interaction with my mother was basically saying goodbye to her, which was the hardest thing I have ever had to do in my life. Our limited time to enjoy one another in this world is now limited to one month or less.

My mother's condition worsened day by day, and there was nothing I could do about it. There was no cancer treatment center for pancreatic cancer in Uganda when you are diagnosed with cancer, it's a death sentence. You just have to wait for your time to go to the Lord. There is only one chemotherapy machine for the entire population of about fifty million Ugandans suffering from all forms of cancers, and the machine is almost fifty years old and breaks down all the time, leaving patients who are being treated hanging on when the machine beaks.

People who have been diagnosed with cancer from all walks of life from different parts of Uganda converge in this one hospital called Mulago hospital waiting for their turn to receive chemotherapy for their cancer diagnosis from this one machine. It is heartbreaking to see the level of suffering for the poor people sleeping outside under a tree and veranda of the hospital with nothing to eat and nothing to nurse their wounds. We made the decision to take our mother home so we could be with her in her last moments and give her comfort while she waited for her time to be called by her Father in heaven and because our mother had such a strong faith that she was well prepared to face whatever that will come to her and she was ready.

At first, I didn't know what to do I came from America to fulfill my promise to my mother that I made to her when I was a young child, and now I was faced with the reality that she was remaining with only one month or less to live, it was the hardest thing to face in my life but I have to come to terms with that reality now facing me and accept it and be strong. In my last moments interacting with my mother. She kept asking me, "How is life in America?" whether I was happy living in America because she said that was what her prayer was for me that God should grant me happiness and that she continued to recite the same prayer all the time when she could not see me face to face. She wanted me to find happiness and achieve the goals that had brought me to America and my mother told me she prayed that I should continue to help the poor wherever I may be because it true and Godly way of living a better life and that is the Christian way of leading a better life by helping in need.

I was touched by my mother's words to me and when I told her I was working with an organization called Catholic Charities, that helped poor and vulnerable populations in poor communities in America. My mother was touched and blessed me more and said to me that is what God wants me to do and that I should continue to do good for the people around the world and I would be rewarded for doing good for people. The last thing that my mother told me was that I should not forget about the poor children in Africa because I was once upon a time those children and God heard our prayers and led me away from that suffering and now it was my time to give back to God's children in Africa and give back to the hungry children going to bed with no food or water in our community in Uganda or in Africa as a whole.

I could not hold my tears when I heard these words from my mother and I wanted to ask my mother the question of how I would be able to fulfill this monumental task that she had put before me, but then I remembered what she told me way back as a young man growing up poor in our rural village in Adwila that there is nothing I couldn't do if I work hard for it and put my trust in God to guide me through.

Before her final day in this world, my mother still made sure that the community children that she was by providing with food and drink would be continued to be fed and her final wish for me was to request that I continue to feed those poor children in our community, and my heart was touched by my mother caring heart even at the final hour of her life. She still had that compassionate heart for the poor people in my community. I was humbled and proud to be the son of such a caring mother who had such a kind heart for humankind.

My mother's caring heart attracted many poor children in our community to our home because they knew when they get to our home they will be fed and given drink and it was an amazing thing to see our compound was always full of children lined up and playing at our home by witnessing the humble and simple life my mother led her life made life worth living. My mother made sure she had a purpose for living in this world. She found her calling in this world and made sure she fulfilled her calling with no regrets.

Within two days, my mother passed away peacefully on her bed surrounded by her twelve children with many grandchildren in her little iron sheet house built by the beloved precious baby boy that God blessed her with to deliver her and the family and the community from the evil of poverty. When the news of my mother passing away was received in the community, I observed the flocking of many children from our community to our compound with tears on their faces, and I was surprised and asked my sisters where are all these children coming from and who are they? And I remember my sisters telling me these are the children your mother was feeding with the $50 you send to her monthly to feed herself but instead she was feeding up this multitude of children in her community because these children have nowhere to go and find food and drink. Their mothers and fathers are very poor and have no means to take care of them so your mother has been taking care of them, and now they have received the news of her passing away, and they are coming to pay their respects, and they are crying because they did know where and who will continue to feed them.

At that moment, I didn't know what to do with these children. I knew my mother told me before her passing to continue to take care of the children she was feeding at her home, but I didn't know they were all that many so when I saw all these many children coming to our home and need food because they were so hungry. I was shocked but not surprised because this is where I grew up, and I knew my community people were very poor but being that I have not lived in my village for fifteen years, I didn't fully understand the current situation in my childhood community. Also, because I had lived in the country of plenty America for fifteen years and become complacent and comfortable seeing this level of suffering by children just blew my mind.

I immediately started thinking if this were America I would work with the restaurants and the local supermarkets to bring to these children much-needed food from what went to waste and was thrown out every day. All kinds of thoughts came to my mind and keep thinking about how to address the suffering of these children and how could I match up with what my mother was doing to help these children. It was a big challenge, for sure, but I knew eventually I would figure out what I needed to do to help these children but at that moment I needed to focus on how I will give a decent burial and a good send off for my mother who had sacrificed her entire life caring for me and my sisters and my brothers to make sure we have a better life than theirs.

My mother was everything to me they did all that needed to be done to care of their children under a very difficult circumstance, they did not abandon their twelve children. Instead, they sacrifice their all lives to take care of their children, so it was our turn just to say thank you for what you have done for us and the people in our community, and we owe you so much, and I hope I will emulate all that you did for us and taught us, and we will continue to instill that great message of good deeds to our own children to improve the lives around us and the lives around the world and make the world a better place to live regardless of one economic status.

When the time came to say goodbye to our mother, I saw tears coming rolling down the cheeks of these malnourished children, and I wondered why they were crying and what was going through their minds. Although I will never know what was in their thoughts, I did know the children's unconditional love for my mother, and they knew they will never see my mother again, and that also gave me the strength and courage, knowing that my mother was much-loved by other people, and she did her job well as a mother, and it was time for her to go and rest peacefully. We sang my mother's favorite song to say goodbye to her, and wish that God be with her until we met again while we lowered her coffin to the grave, and I kept thinking my mother was so proud of me because we did such a great job for being there for at her final days, and she was smiling looking down upon us and saying, "You, my children, I love you all," and that feeling gave me peace of mind that I was there for my mother at her last time on this earth, even though I had not seen her for all that many years.

When the time was ready to say goodbye to my community and my sisters and brothers, I was very emotional I didn't want to leave them because we built such a strong bond again like when we were young, but I had to returned to America to be with my four children, who were in my heart the whole time. On my way to the airport and onto the plane, I kept thinking about what I should do to continue to feed the poor children I left behind that my mother was taking care of and knew this is what I wanted to do for the rest of my life to care for the poor and the vulnerable population in Uganda and eventually all of Africa. But how to begin this difficult task, but I know I love challenges in my life, and this will be one of them, and one of the ideas that came to my mind was to start a nonprofit organization that would help the poor children in Uganda, and the second idea was to write a book about life and the challenges I faced growing up and the proceeds I got from the book, I would use it to care for the poor children in my community and Uganda children as a whole, but the challenges I faced in accomplishing this goal was because I had a full-time job to take care of my family, so I don't have enough time to dedicate myself fully to run a nonprofit job or to sit down and write a book, but I know one day I would be able to overcome those challenges and do what I love to do to work with the poor and the vulnerable population.

That time came in March 2020, when the global pandemic Covid-19 hit the entire world and businesses around the world came to a standstill, and we were all laid off from our fulltime jobs. I knew straight away this is the time for me to sit down and write my book with the hope I would be able to do what I wanted to do for a long time to help the suffering children in Uganda in my community and all of Uganda children.

I hope to be able to change the lives of many children around the world and bring smiles to their faces by starting from Uganda and expanding to other nations. I want to be the voice for the voiceless poor children around the world like I was once before, but now that I have seen the light and come out of that darkness and am empowered more than ever to do good things to change the lives of many suffering children around the world. I hope my story will open your heart and examine your heart and touched your heart and gives you comfort to your heart whatever what you are going through in your life and know that those are the challenges of the world we are all born in this world and face different forms of challenges in our lifetimes, but we should never give up hope when we are faced with those difficult challenges. I am not saying it would be easy, but I am saying let's face our challenges with determination and hope that someday you will overcome all those challenges before you, and you will become a better person learning from those challenges you went through.

My hope that you will be so kind to whoever is close to your life when you are going through this difficult time in your life, and I hope by reading this book it will help you along the way to know that you are not alone whatever challenges you may be going through and to know those challenges may be temporary. There are better days ahead of you, so please never give up continue to fight on to overcome the difficulties you're facing, be they financial difficulties, marital difficulties, poverty, and you cannot put food on the table and the children are crying looking into your eyes and want something to eat please know that you are not alone and that those challenges are temporal someday you will overcome them.

I hope you find peace and comfort and enjoyment in your life after going through so much, and I hope you follow your dreams in terms of what you want to do with your life after going through so much in life after facing so much adversity. My prayer to you is that you never leave God out of your life when going through difficult times. It's only God who can lean on in times of despair and hopelessness. I hope you find peace after going through challenging times and purpose and meaning and that you lead a healthy life without the fear, and I hope my story will strengthen you and make you a stronger person and encourage you to do more good to one another and be your brothers and sisters' keepers in time they need you most, and I hope my story will encourage you to be the voice for the meek and the voiceless people in the community where you leave, and I hope my story will allow you to look at yourself and your heart to do good to people you even don't know and I hope you will be encouraged to give more of what you have if you can afford to bless the lives of less fortunate people around your community and you will be blessed. And I hope my story will encourage you to even work harder to achieve whatever goal set is ahead of you and above all be who you are and love yourself no matter what your economic status is do not be ashamed or afraid of yourself from asking for help and advice to keep you moving on and know you are loved and be blessed. Do not let your economic status be a stumbling block in front of you or an excuse as to why you cannot achieve what you really want to achieve in life. I refuse to be defined by my poverty brought up as a child, but I am proud of who I am today and I am proud of my heritage and my community in northern Uganda, and it is now my time to see that I improve the lives in my community and build them the school to send their children to school to gain the knowledge their children desperately need and to build the hospital they desperately need to treat the sick and the dying.

Photo: My older brother Nixon Okello with his eight children along with the children in Adwila that my mother was supporting before her death.

Photo: My beloved mother Bensy Apio and my beloved father Naputal Ogwang sitting down with their last-born child Geoffrey Ojok. Sitting in their house their son Vincent Ajuk built for them, keeping his promise to them after his education. My father loved my mother unconditionally and we all twelve children grew up loving them back unconditionally.

Photo: My beloved mother in her house on her final year on earth when she was diagnosed with pancreatic cancer and there was no where she could get treatment in Uganda. I to her to get treatment in Uganda hospital, but I could not find where to get cancer treatment. My heart was broken as a son to see your mother suffering, and there was nothing you can do to help her with her pain and suffering. The iron rod mother and our rock to our family was now about to say goodbye to her beloved twelve children and go to heaven to reunite with her creator God and Jesus Christ who she had strong faith that guided her during very had times when she was completely living in abject poverty.

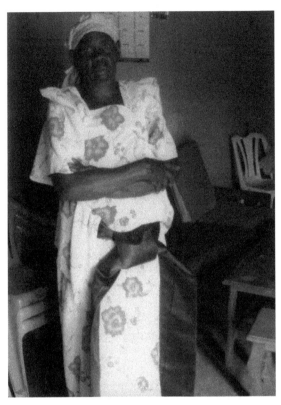

Photo: The picture of my beloved mother in her house her son Vincent Ajuk built for her. This picture was taken just after she was told she had pancreatic cancer. The news was so devasting for my mother after suffering so much to raise her twelve children in abject poverty and when it was time for her son Vincent Ajuk to take care of her and enjoy a little bit of happiness, and now she had to face the news of debilitating disease that will take her life. My mother was motionless and confused and did not know what to do with the news, but as always, she was a very strong women with strong faith in God, and because of her strong faith, nothing could shake her up.

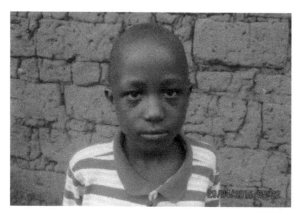

Photo: *A young boy name Ajuk, my namesake, in our community that my mother was feeding and taking care. I took his picture in front our mud grass thatch house in 2015 to remind me of when I was young like him and had nothing but because our mother and father sacrificed for me and gave me the chance to pursue my goal in education to have a better life. I wanted to keep this picture to remind me always to do good and give him a chance in life to pursue his education and have a better life. This picture reminds me while in America to not to forget where I came from and share with all those kids who are suffering in our community with the little that God has blessed me with.*

Photo: *This picture of young Odongo reminds me of our mud grass thatch house I grew up in. I took the picture on my recent trip in our village in northern Uganda Lira district to visit the home I grew up loving and the memory that comes with it. The structure is well maintained by his mother, smeared with cow dung and black soil to keep it clean all the time free of disease.*

Faith and Family:
Growing up Poor in Rural Uganda

Photo: The author, Vincent Ajuk. Home in America, what I term "the power of education." Without education none of this would have been possible for a child who grew up in abject poverty in Lira rural Uganda.

Photo: The proud father Vincent Ajuk attending the university graduation of his older son Elvis Ogwang along with his three children Allan Ajuk, Apio Phiona, and Alele Patricia.

About the Author

Vincent Ajuk was born in the village of Adwila in the Lira district of Uganda to the family of Naputal Ogwang and. Bensy Apio. He had fourteen siblings, but two died at birth, leaving Vincent with eleven siblings, eight sisters and three brothers. Large families were not unusual in the African communities of Vincent's region where they were means of protection and help support the family as labor. Vincent's parents were poor, and it was very difficult to raise their twelve children on the money raised from growing cotton, sugar cane, tomatoes, and vegetables.

The family lived in a thatched-grass, mud hut without running water or electricity. Vincent's family used the small income they raised from selling their agricultural output to buy things like soap, salt, and used clothes. Conditions required that the children traveled long distances to collect clean drinking water for home use. The parents shared a strong Christian faith and instilled Christian values and faith in all their children. Vincent's parents had no formal education, but they had a passion for educating their twelve children, not wanting to see their children face their fate. His parents knew the value of education, and they wanted their children to attend school. His mother was an ardent supporter of girls' education, and she wanted her girls to have the opportunities that she'd been denied by her father.

Vincent's father knew the only way they would be able to produce enough food to feed the family and get sufficient excess to the local market for sale to earn income to pay for the children's education was to engage them in family farming. At an early age, the parents taught their children the value of hard work by teaching them to yolk oxen to plow the land for growing cotton and vegetables. They attended school only after working the fields, so often went hungry and sometimes had to make it through the day on water alone, and even that was difficult to obtain. After school, the siblings would help their parents with the domestic chores.

Vincent attended secondary school at the Dr. Joseph Obote College. When he received his secondary school degree, he attended the Uganda College of Commerce in Apac where he studied accounting. Initially, he was unable to find a position as an accountant until he made a fortunate connection through his brother-in-law, and he was able to secure a position as a bookkeeper. Upon receiving employment in Kampala as a business professional. Vincent understood that his first responsibility was to repay his parents for their sacrifices and to honor his sisters who were forced to stay at home. He built them a solid house with a metal roof and a permanent water source. This is a classic portrait of how education can improve the lives of rural Ugandans.

He continued to work hard to provide for his family and community, though the northern region of Uganda faced many hardships, including cattle rustling and the incursion of the Lord Resistance Army. Led by Joseph Kony, this loosely organized paramilitary unit wreaked untold horrors upon the people of Uganda, including murder, kidnapping, and rape. Among these statistics was Vincent's niece who was abducted by the rebels from a Catholic secondary school.

In 2000, Vincent decided that he wanted to raise his children in peace and security, and he knew the place to do this was America. That year, he emigrated to the United States. Adapting to a new country in which he knew only his young children, Vincent he enrolled in St. Joseph's University in Philadelphia to pursue a Bachelor of Science degree in Business Management/Accounting while working two full-time jobs as a single father to support his four children.

He was hired by the non-profit Catholic Charities, Diocese of Camden, as Director of Welfare where he worked with poor and vulnerable populations. This work reinforced his determination to help the poor.

In 2007, Vincent founded a nonprofit organization American Friends of Northern Uganda (www.afonu.org)to help the poor and disadvantaged peoples in the rural communities of Uganda, including providing clean drinking water, funding children's education, and feeding orphaned children in Uganda.

These goals have long been Vincent's passion because he understands the role education played in his life and wants to ensure young men and young women in poor communities around the world get the education that will change their lives and their families.

Printed in the USA
CPSIA information can be obtained
at www.ICGtesting.com
LVHW071833251023
761973LV00019B/279/J

9 781737 114406